ANGELS UNAWARES

ANGELS UNAWARES

Megan McKenna

Paulist Press
New York / Mahwah NJ

Cover image by heyoka/Bigstock.com
Cover design by Dawn Massa, Lightly Salted Graphics
Book design by Lynn Else

First published by Orbis Books. Copyright © 1995 by Megan McKenna
This edition published in 2015 by Paulist Press, Inc.

Unless otherwise noted, biblical translations are from the *Christian Community Bible, 8th Edition* (Claretian Publications, 1991).

Material on Mount Saint Michael's in Chapter 1 was gleaned from "The Beautiful Legends of Mount Saint Michael in French, German, Spanish, English," Bureau des Annales, F50116, Le Mont Saint-Michel, Avranches, 1990 edition. "St. Peter and the Angel" is from *Oblique Prayers*. Copyright © 1984 by Denise Levertov. Reprinted by permission of New Directions Publishing Corp. and Gerald Pollinger, Ltd., 18 Maddox St., Mayfair, London W1R 0EU United Kingdom. Further permissions to reprint previously published material may be found on p. 179.

Library of Congress Cataloging-in-Publication Data

McKenna, Megan.
    Angels unawares / Megan McKenna.
       pages cm
    ISBN 978-0-8091-4896-7 (pbk. : alk. paper) — ISBN 978-1-58768-419-7 (ebook)
    1. Angels—Christianity. I. Title.
    BT966.2.M36 2014
    235'.3—dc23

                                                                    2014034142

ISBN 978-0-8091-4896-7 (paperback)
ISBN 978-1-58768-419-7 (e-book)

Published by Paulist Press
997 Macarthur Boulevard
Mahwah, New Jersey 07430

www.paulistpress.com

Printed and bound in the United States of America

For the dear ones the Holy One has sent to me,
my long-distance angels,
Pat, Celeste, Maria
and the sisters of the Carmelite Monastery,
Reno, Nevada,
who pray me home and pray for those
who listen to my stories.

And for my computer angels,
brothers and monks, Ben, Joseph and Jeff,
without whose help this book
would never have been written.

May the angels keep you company,
sing to you
and give you visions
of the new heaven and new earth
you so fervently long for
and seek with your prayers and lives.

CONTENTS

PREFACE

The first time I encountered an "angel's kiss" was in Llangollen, Wales, this past year. It was dusk with a wild swirl of sky, storms and near night. The angel's kiss was warm and tasted of fire; I sighed before every sip. This angel's kiss: two parts brandy to one part Benedictine.

The next day wandering the wet Welsh hills we found an old church, the Chapel of Rug. Its garden was blooming with medieval plants, one called angel's blush. I took seeds to plant half a world away in New Mexico.

Then, the very next night in Liverpool, we had angel hair pasta and angel food cake! What is this universal enchantment and fascination with angels?

Looking through manuscript collections in the National Gallery in London I found an angel with a millstone (from the Apocalypse) "reducing every grain of separate existence to the dust of divine union" at the end of time. From the early Middle Ages, there were angels surrounding a book in a garden, studying it with diligence and reverence. I also saw an angel as the axis of the world, holding the world in place in obedience to love (from a ninth-century mosaic in the vault of the Church of Santa Prassede, Rome). Again, in a parish church from the 1800s in England I stood among a choir of angels with peacock-feather wings the colors of twilight, sentinels and watchers of the kingdom of earth.

In pamphlets on the Shrine of Fatima, Michael the Archangel is named the guardian angel of Portugal and the precursor of the visit of Mary to the three children. In the Convent of Aviron on Mt. Athos in Greece, John the Baptist, barefoot and clad in skins, joins the choirs of angels, for he is the angel of Jesus, going before to prepare for the Word. Mary, as the queen of angels, is honored especially, for "she is the true throne of God and thus she exalts the thrones of God."

And then there is Raphael, often painted as companion to young men leaving for war or off to make their fortunes in the world. These paintings were given as gifts to mothers, assuring them of divine protection and accompaniment for their sons.

St. Bede tells the story of Caedmon, who began life unable to utter a word. In the evenings the villagers would pass the harp around and sing. Caedmon would steal off to the woods in shame, longing to pray and suffer apart from all the shared companionship and passing on of tradition and hope in story and music. One night an angel appeared to him and commanded him to sing. His lips, tongue and vocal cords were unsealed, and he became a poet and great bard.

In Native American tradition, Lame Deer, a holy man of the Sioux, describes four thunderbirds with wings, beaks and claws. As descriptions of Ezekiel's visitors that attend the presence of God, they are at home in this layered world of spirit.

In many traditions angels are involved with language: with creation stories, the workings of the universe, in music, chants, poetry and prayer, in the repositories of meaning, memories and hope. The bard, poet and priest are touched by angels. All those things with wings—dances of words, poetic meters, drums, strings, woodwinds, plainsong—all are bound to tales of angels. They are gifts, moments and notes grounded in eternity. The Sufi believe that each of the letters of the Arabic alphabet is ruled by an angel. Words, inner meanings and interpretations are the domain of angels. In fact, the word for "angel" among the Sufis is the same as their word for icon—a window for the soul into the world beyond the veils that barely separate us from the divine.

And place. Michael is partial to mountains, to magnificent vistas of scenery and equally magnificent architecture, as Mount Saint Michael and Michael's Mount. This archangel is patron of Israel, Portugal, Brittany, Cornwall, the Nile in Egypt, El Salvador. Snowy, mountainous shrines in Germany are dedicated to him. He lingers near caves and is attracted to dragons—not to destroy or eliminate them but to tame, leash, order and use their powers toward spiritual ends. Each land and nation is believed to have its own angel.

In Enoch (who is thought to be an angel himself by many, as he is taken to walk with God forever), four angels are presented by name: Michael, the merciful and long suffering; Raphael, set over diseases and wounds of the children of earth; Gabriel, set over all the powers, especially word and revelation; and Phanuel, set over the repentance and hope of those who inherit eternal life (and so, set over death as well). This last angel, sometimes called Ariel or Azrael, is veiled in a thousand veils before creatures and holds between his hands immensity. He often has four faces, one before, one on his head, one beneath his feet, and one behind, and innumerable eyes. When one eye closes, it is said, someone dies.

Angels are associated with ends, judgments, reckonings. They obey and execute God's decisions and the results of our choices, escorting souls to heaven or thrusting them into hell. They divide the vaults of heaven in the domes of churches into four, inviting the soul to contemplation and union with the divine, becoming lost in all things, disappearing into adoration, in communion and union with God. They form ladders, ascending and descending, and are given the souls of humans to care for and lead to God. "It is a teaching of Moses that every believer has an angel to guide him as a teacher and a shepherd" (St. Basil).

The story of Jacob's ladder in Genesis has echoes of this conjunction of place and spirituality. Joseph "was afraid and said, 'How full of awe is this place! It is nothing less than a House of God; it is the Gate to Heaven'" (Gen. 28:17). These thresholds are the places of angels. As St. John Chrysostom reminds us,

> that spiritual ladder which the patriarch Jacob saw stretches from earth to heaven. The angels were coming down along it and the martyrs were going up. You have often seen the sun rise in the morning, darting out purple-tinted rays in every direction. Such were the bodies of the martyrs: the crimson tide of their blood had flooded every part of them as with rays of purple and illuminated their bodies more than the sun lights up the heaven. The angels gazed upon this book with delight!

It seems that prophets, martyrs and mystics are close kin to angels.

Angels announce births and attend ascension. Milton says they have to fight and resist with great effort to stay down. They rise, fly, appear in trances, visions and dreams. They lift souls in ecstasy and take up Elijah in his fiery-wheeled chariot. They rise with Jesus (who, tradition says, left his footprint lingering on the hill) and question those left looking up to heaven—gawking—"Why are you looking up to heaven?" Now the Presence resides on earth in the Spirit's children, until the coming of the kingdom.

The ceiling of the church of Debre Berken in Ethiopia pictures a system of ascending levels of reality like the rungs of a ladder: physical, mental, psychic, spiritual and finally total union with the Divine where all reality is holy. And an angel is encountered at each stage or rung of the ladder, as guardian of the threshold. That angel teaches or initiates the meaning of the experience within it to the pilgrim soul.

Angels are creatures of ethereal loveliness but also represent an almost terrifying vision of ultimate Truth. They rarely resemble fat, playful cherubs; more often they are flaming swords unsheathed, intimations of the Holy One who made them, pieces of transcendence drawing near. They are universal it seems, almost familiar, but uncannily strange, disturbing even to one such as Mary. They tear the heart out of time, alter the pattern, demand the aid of humans. They are, simply, servants of the Lord.

Angels, mysteries of God's imagination, invitations to obedience and servants visiting earth, are the Creator's call to each of us to reconsider, change, be transformed. They urge us to turn again toward each other and love. They watch and wait for us at home, knowing we are crucial to the heart of God incarnate. They care about us and come to visit and deliver God's word to us. These angels of God are envelopes waiting for our replies.

ON STORYTELLING

What is a story? For the one who tells the tale, it is truth shared. For the one who hears it told, it is an invitation, a lure deep into universal experience. Once told, it echoes and is remembered a bit differently by all who listened. It is mercurial, liquid, fluid. But take the story out of the teller's mouth and put it down on the page and the form is altered radically. It becomes solid, cast in ink and paper that, as in days of old, could just as well have been carved in stone. That is when the issue arises of whether a story—or a version of it—can be owned and copyrighted.

Most of the stories found in my books were told by me after being heard; a few I have told after having seen a printed version of them. Stories take on a life of their own in the telling. A printed version is often more stilted. Oftentimes there are various written versions, old and new, some adapted from other written versions and some adapted from another's oral telling. When I am aware of a written version, I try to include a reference to it, but my text is usually closer to how I tell the story rather than to any written version. Most of the stories I tell are available on tape, and these versions are closer to the original meaning and intent.

Many storytellers believe that there is only One Story, that all others serve that One and that no individual owns the words. I belong to this group wholeheartedly. I always tell where the story belongs, its source in tradition, and who gave it to me, if I know. I hand it on, as it has been given to me, as freely as I can.

INTRODUCTION

Angels? Just what do we believe about angels? According to the scriptures, angels appear in a variety of roles and activities. They are guardians of nations, sanctuaries, churches, holy places and of each individual. They are worshipers of God as well as God's companions, messengers, protectors, watchers and witnesses. In the Hebrew scriptures they are called the host of heaven, a court, the Sons of Elohim (in Job and Psalm 29 and Daniel). In the letters of Paul and Peter angels are connected with the cosmic order and with social forces that may be hostile to the gospel. No matter how they are described, the "principalities and powers," the angels, are always subject to Christ and always obey the word of God.

It is Christ who is the center of the angelic world. The angels serve him, belong to him, worship and praise him; their songs and praise resound throughout the church's liturgy and public prayer. Just as Jesus' life was filled with angels—prior to his birth, at his coming into the world and again at his leaving—angels are present in the life of the church and with believers in the crucial moments of birth, baptism, struggles with temptations and evil, and at death. St. Thomas writes: "The angels work together for the benefit of us all."

Near the entrance of a Catholic seminary in the United States, there is an old weathered statue of a guardian angel. It stands, stone-still, grimy with age and the elements, pious, hovering beside and protective of a young child. I heard a strange story about it from one of the seminarians.

- A man, obviously profoundly retarded—or close to the truth—came to visit: he had wandered away from a nearby institution. He saw the angel and climbed up beside it and hung there caressing the angel's hard sculptured, cold face. Sensuously, tenderly, in public but oblivious to all. He stayed there for hours. No one moved toward him, questioned him, cared for him. Some who passed by watched, laughed, made fun of him. Eventually his caretakers found him and took him away. A nobody who touched an angel standing forlornly in a monastery garden.

The angel statue is still there so I went to see it. Where is the man who fingered an angel's face? Does the angel guard and protect him now? Does the angel tenderly, softly caress his face with thanks? Did the gawkers miss the mystery enacted before their eyes and knowingly walk away from two angels caught unawares, communicating in the light of an almost spring day? The story makes me unbearably sad and longing. Am I too seeking an angel?

The belief in angels has been an ancient and honored tradition of the church from its earliest days and struggles. According to medieval tradition it was on the first day of creation that angels were made, crafted of light by the Holy One and found to be good.

In the beginning, when God began to create the heavens and the earth, the earth had no form and was void; darkness was over the deep and the Spirit of God hovered over the waters. God said, "Let there be light"; and there was light. God saw that the light was good and he separated the light from the darkness. (Gen. 1:1–4)

In the final book of the Christian scriptures, Revelation, we hear of other beginnings that are also part of the common belief: the war in heaven between the opposing forces of angels.

War broke out in heaven with Michael and his angels battling with the dragon. The dragon fought back with his angels, but they were defeated and lost their place in heaven. The great dragon, the ancient serpent known as the devil or Satan, seducer of the whole world, was thrown out. He was hurled down to earth, together with his angels. (Rev. 12:7–9)

It is here that we truly begin, with this war in heaven. What caused this war? Dissension in heaven? In-fighting among pure spirits of light? What could possibly be at its root? The early Fathers of the church, medieval philosophers, folk wisdom and morality tales all concur: the angels themselves were tested, were asked to choose their relationship to God freely.

This is the old tradition, told in stories and legends and spiritual treatises. Some of the angels refused to obey the will of God and honor Adam, the first human created by God. They refused to bend before someone they considered beneath them. In so doing, they refused to bend before God who, in the divine plan hidden from the beginning, would come among us as one like us, subject to trial, suffering and death, even death on a cross. These angels refused to honor the wisdom of God, which would be revealed in the creation of human beings and fulfilled in the mystery of the Incarnation, God becoming the least of our brothers and sisters, human and vulnerable, and yet revealing God in ways unimagined and unheard of by the angels.

In the New Testament when Paul writes of angels he is adamant about God's closeness with human beings in the person of the beloved, Jesus Christ, who is obedient, firstborn and Son. For Paul there is no comparison between the angels and Jesus; the angels are servants of God sent to help those of us who shall be saved. Angels worship God by helping humankind be saved. This is part of the infinite plan of God, hidden from the beginning but revealed gloriously, strangely, compassionately in Jesus.

Paul goes on to describe this new world ushered in by the life, death and resurrection of Jesus:

The angels were not given dominion over the new world of which we are speaking. Instead someone declared in Scripture: What is man, that you should be mindful of him? For a while you placed him a little lower than the angels, but you crowned him with glory and honor. You have given him dominion over all things.... But Jesus who suffered death and for a little while was placed lower than the angels has been crowned with honor and glory. For the merciful plan of God demanded that he experience death on behalf of everyone.... This is why his death destroyed the one holding the power of death, that is the devil, and freed those who remained in bondage all their lifetime because of the fear of death. Jesus came to take by the hand not the angels but the human race.... Having been tested through suffering, he is able to help those who are tested. (Heb. 2:5–9, 14–16, 18)

It is in this tradition that the fall of the angels is seen: that on the day God created the first human being out of dust drawn from the soil, and breathed into his nostrils the breath of life, and he became alive, the angels were tested. Those who remained obedient to God were entrusted with the care and the protection of earth and human beings, and the battle that began in the realm of the spirit would continue on earth in flesh and blood, in the history of humankind.

Contrary to our usual images of winged creatures, those obedient angels who watch over us are bodiless. While some are known to us by name in a familiar way, angels are distinguished from one another by function rather than by material characteristics. There are traditionally nine orders of angels in three hierarchical sets: the highest are the cherubim, seraphim and thrones; next come dominations, virtues and powers; and the lowest orders are the principalities, archangels and angels. It is these lowest orders that we feel we know so well. The four archangels most known by name in the Western church are Michael, Gabriel, Raphael and Ariel (or Phanuel). The Eastern churches name three additional archangels: Selephiel, the archangel of wisdom; Varachiel, the guardian of truth and courage in the face of persecution and opposition; and Yegovdiel, the angel of unity, who knows all the languages of the world and its creatures.

How do we describe an angel? Perhaps we can best describe angels by what they do rather than by how they look. Angels instill in those who see them or hear them a violent need to obey the Truth. Since they stand always in awe before God and worship God, no matter what else they have been charged with doing, that presence of the Holy exudes from them. Sometimes angels have been described as ways by which human beings apprehend the presence, the knowledge and the will of God.

While angels are as attentive to God as they are to us humans, they are bound also to earth, water, air and fire. They stir waters that heal and they are guardian spirits of places of refuge and safe haven. They wrestle with us, like Jacob, and leave us limping but with a blessing. They struggle and teach us how to do battle with spirit as well as flesh.

They may bring unsettling visions, sights, and knowledge that is crucial and disturbing to the human psyche and spirit, but necessary for humankind's survival. They are offended by violence and horrified by the death of the innocent. It is said that angels weep when we make God weep again, as Jesus sweated blood and cried out in a garden on a warm spring night long ago.

Angels are evidence that God is taking notice of us. They ask the same always: surrender, obedience, submission, radical abasement and humility before the Holy One. Some say they make us homesick for heaven. They are always present, ministering, even though we are unaware of them. They hover near wombs, caves, gardens and tombs, but almost any place is made holy by their visitation. They stand in silent rage against inhumanity, knowing that it is up to us to oppose it, not them. They love earth even more since the Incarnation, and they come to visit and linger in the houses of the poor, in the byways and on the roads. They seem always to be asking us to make alliance with them and so comfort God, who has come to save us all and restore earth to the original dream of holiness. As the angels retie the bonds between heaven and earth, the mysterious plan from the beginning will be fulfilled.

The rejoicing of the angels at Jesus' ascension is part of the restoration of human beings to God's original harmony and order. That restoration is described in the Book of Revelation in glowing terms of elation, sunlight, glory and promises fulfilled in intimacy with God. The universe will be at one again because of the atonement of Jesus Christ and those who chose his kingdom of heaven on earth. The angels of light greet the person of Jesus, human and divine, as the promise of God triumphing over Satan's futile deceits.

Thus, the angels are bound up with us and our choices for good and evil, now and always. The end and the beginning are connected, and the place where they meet is in the person of Jesus Christ. It is part of the mystery of God's ways that began in Genesis and continues now. We are meant to fear evil, to fight and confront evil, as the serpent confronted our ancestors and still confronts us. We are meant to align ourselves with the angels of light, with Jesus Christ and all those who struggle against the shadows of evil until we meet in the New Jerusalem.

MICHAEL THE ARCHANGEL

Protector

God posted cherubim and a flaming sword that kept turning at the east of the garden of Eden to guard the way to the tree of Life.

—Genesis 3:24

In medieval legends this sword is wielded by Michael, an archangel, a member of the lowest order of angels, which consists of principalities, archangels and angels. This order has been put in charge of human hierarchies and history. Its members are the guardians of the tree of Life, which is Jesus, the glory of God, hung upon the tree of the cross, which is the doorway to the kingdom of God, to life everlasting.

Michael, first named of the angels, and Gabriel, named in the Book of Daniel, will be friends and close allies of humankind. Even though Michael is stationed by God at the entrance to the garden with a fiery revolving sword to keep us from entering until the proper time, he also is charged with being the protector of the people of God. The legends about Michael all echo hope and reflect the experience of those who believe not in a God to fear and hide from, but a God who cares, saves and mysteriously can restore and redeem even choices of evil.

This is one of those legends:

• Once upon a time…really before our time began, after the war in heaven when Satan and his followers were cast forth from the abiding presence of the Light, Michael the archangel was commissioned by God to defend the earth and take charge of the garden where Yahweh God would place Adam and Eve.

Just as he had obeyed God and bowed before the image of the Maker of all things, Michael obeyed and went immediately to guard the Garden of Eden. For, it is believed that Yahweh God knew of Satan's intent to destroy creation, to upset the harmony and balance of the earth, and to distort the plan of God to lift humankind up from its lowly place below the angels to be God's own friends and children. So God sent Michael to be on the lookout for Satan and to protect our ancestors from their choice and fate as exiles cast forth from the presence of God. But Michael failed.

The angel once known as Lucifer, now Satan, was crafty, sly and devious. He changed form, coming into the garden as a serpent (not a snake, more like a dragon or other fantastic creature). And so it was that Michael, unsuspecting, let him slip by. Thus Satan entrapped Adam and Eve, and they fell from grace and glory. Michael was expecting a creature, an angel of light like the one that he battled in the heavens, not one of the wild creatures that Yahweh God had made.

When Adam and Eve and all their offspring were exiled from Eden, Yahweh God stationed Michael with the flaming revolving sword at the gate of the garden, charging him to keep them from entering again. And so Michael obeyed. But Michael was crushed, brokenhearted that he had failed God's charge. He had not been able to prevent Adam and Eve from sinning; he had not protected the people of God.

He stood guard, and yet he had pity on Adam and Eve, who now had to toil and sweat, work and suffer just to survive, and then to die. Yahweh God had made for them garments of skin and clothed them so that they did not go naked into the world, and so Michael thought to give a gift to Adam and Eve as well. In pity for the wretchedness of their lives, Michael took his flaming sword and transformed it into a plow, teaching Adam to till the fields and bring forth food from the land. Thus he eased their burden and his own sense of failing God and the people of God.

They say that ever since then Michael has been the defender of the honor of God. Like God, he cares for the poor and the lowliest of the earth, the ones who plow the fields and harvest the crops and provide food for others. He defends and guards as patron all those who struggle against evil face to face, confronting it and seeking to stop its power in their flesh and lives.

They say too that Michael was the first to learn that one cannot fight evil on earth as one does in heaven, and that Michael is the first proponent of nonviolent resistance to evil. It is Michael's experience of Satan on earth that is remembered and echoed and given substance in all the visions, hopes and promises of the prophets, specifically:

In the last days, the mountain of Yahweh's house shall be set over the highest mountains and shall tower over the hills.

All the nations shall stream to it, saying, "Come, let us go to the mountain of the Lord, to the house of the God of Jacob, that he may teach us his ways and we may walk in his paths." For the Teaching comes from Zion, and from Jerusalem the word of Yahweh.

He will rule over the nations and settle disputes for many peoples. They will beat their swords into plowshares and their spears into pruning hooks. Nation will not raise sword against nation; they will train for war no more. (Isa. 2:2–5)

Christ, who climbed the mountain of the transfiguration and the mount of Calvary, is the hinge uniting the meaning of creation and all humankind's history. Michael and all the angels of God are sent to us to accompany us through suffering and to the restoration of the glory of God. All the stories of Michael remind us of the honor of God, obedience to God, trusting in God's wisdom and submitting to the mysteries of the Incarnation, the cross and the resurrection. They tell of Michael's presence with the victims of evil and injustice; he stands with those who stand against evil, especially the prophets, martyrs and the poor. In many places, Michael the archangel is called the patron of liberation theologians and all those who speak on behalf of those with no voice. He stands with all those who speak out against the wisdom of the world, which extols money, power, nationalism, militarism, hate, greed, insensitivity to others, war and violence. Michael stands against the savagery of the human race and the destruction inherent in disobedience.

We read in the Book of Daniel that Michael is the protector and defender of the people of God, of Israel, the one who fights for them in history. In a vision Gabriel tells Daniel: "Michael has come to my assistance" (Dan. 10:13) and "No one lends me support in all this except Michael, your angel" (Dan. 10:21). The Book of Daniel was written around 164 BCE and is the last of the books of the Hebrew Bible. It is part of the Apocrypha, composed during a time of severe crisis for the Jewish people. From this time onward the Jewish communities ascribe certain angels to each of the nations with which they deal. Just as guardian spirits are given to each individual, each nation is assigned a guardian angel in history, and Michael is revealed as Israel's guardian angel. These guardians lend their strength and presence in the struggle between good and evil forces.

In the Hebrew scriptures there are a number of references to the

"Angel of Yahweh." In some of these cases there are hints that the angel involved is Michael because references have to do with swords, violence and fighting using justice and the strength of God. The first and most famous is found in Genesis in the account of the testing of Abraham.

Yahweh God commands Abraham to offer his beloved son, born of his and Sarah's old age in fulfillment of God's promise. Isaac is a child born of God's word, and now it appears that God wants him back as a holocaust, a burnt offering. With horror, Abraham begins to comply with the command. He takes his son and wood for the fire and his knife; he lays his son upon the altar. He stretches out his hand to seize the knife, but the Angel of Yahweh calls to him from heaven: "Abraham! Abraham!" And he says, "Here I am." "Do not lay your hand on the boy; do not harm him, for now I know that you fear God, and you have not held back from me your only son." Abraham looks around and finds a ram for the sacrifice instead, and he offers that to Yahweh. And the Angel of Yahweh calls from heaven a second time,

> By myself I have sworn, it is Yahweh who speaks, because you have done this and not held back your son, your only son, I will surely bless you and make your descendants as numerous as the stars of the sky and the sand on the seashore. Your descendants will take possession of the lands of their enemies. All nations of the earth will be blessed through your descendants because you have obeyed me. (Gen. 22:16–18)

Unfortunately, this story has often been called the sacrifice of Isaac, which, of course, it is not. In the Jewish tradition it is called the binding of Isaac. As problematic as the story is, it reveals one thing clearly: Yahweh God does not want human sacrifice and certainly not the sacrifice of our children. The sacrifice God wants is of mind and heart, obedience to God's word and honoring of God's presence.

The Angel of Yahweh holds back the hand of Abraham and stops him from killing in the name of God, for Yahweh God is the God of the living, of ancestors and history, of families and children through all generations. Abraham, our father in faith, learns this and forever after the people of the promise must be reminded that God is the God of the living. The sword of violence is never to be used in the name of giving worship, sacrifice or honor to God. The angel who conveys this message and revelation from God's own mouth is considered to be Michael the archangel.

This Angel of God also figures strongly in the story of Moses, the liberator of his people. Moses was sent by God into the battle on behalf of the victims of oppression and calculated violence. When he first learns who he really is—a Hebrew and therefore a slave—Moses sees an Egyptian striking a Hebrew and "looking around and seeing no one, he killed the Egyptian and hid him in the sand" (Exod. 2:11–12). Moses has grown up an Egyptian; he is used to violence and, it appears, deceit. This murder is the beginning of Moses' long journey to see God and become obedient to another who uses force but is intent on the life of people, especially innocent and burdened people. Moses has much to learn. He flees from Pharaoh into the desert and then settles in the land of Midian. It is there, while tending his father-in-law's flocks, that he is called by God who "remembered his covenant with Abraham, Isaac and Jacob. God looked upon the sons of Israel and revealed himself to them" (Exod. 2:24f.).

The Angel of Yahweh appeared to him as a flame in the middle of a bush. Moses saw that although the bush was on fire it did not burn up. So Moses goes to see this amazing sight. Then the Angel of Yahweh speaks with the voice of God and reveals to Moses what God is like: God sees the humiliation of the people and hears their cries when they are treated cruelly by their taskmasters. God is both God of the past, of Abraham, Isaac and Jacob, and God of the present: a witness to injustice and inhumanity. God is coming down to free the people and will bring them to a land that will be a secure dwelling place for them. God is liberating, a God who will not tolerate injustice, slavery or pain that is deliberately laid as a burden on human beings by other human beings. God bends toward earth and the cries of those who have no recourse to the powers of this world. When asked to be more specific about what name Moses should use to describe who has sent him to the Israelites, he is told: "I AM WHO I AM...I AM sent me to you." This God is life, being, existence, all that is created, made, sustained, all that can be imagined and more, all that is human and more. This God is fullness of hope and abundant life without end for all generations.

This Angel of Yahweh, speaking forth from a burning bush that is not consumed, lures Moses into the presence of Yahweh. But from this point onward, Yahweh God is at Moses' side and it is Yahweh who takes up the cause of the Israelites and will be the power that Moses yields on behalf of the people. From now on, "Yahweh would speak to Moses face to face, as a man speaks with his neighbor," as spirit to spirit. But it is the Angel of Yahweh who walks before the people and leads the way to the promised land and brings the Israelites to the land of the Amorites, the Hittites, the Perizzites, the Canaanites, the Hivites and the Jebusites (Exod. 23:23).

This Angel of Yahweh also appears to Joshua, and Joshua obeys Yahweh's orders as a soldier would obey a commander, passing on the decrees of Yahweh to the people. This particular story has echoes of Moses and the burning bush and the voice of God telling Moses that where he stands is holy ground.

> When Joshua was near Jericho, he lifted up his eyes and saw before him a man with a drawn sword in his hand. Joshua approached him and said: "Are you for us or for our enemies?" And he answered: "No, I have come as the commander of the army of Yahweh." (Josh. 5:13–14)

In other translations the first words of the angel are clearer, more to the point. He says: "Neither: I am the commander of the army of Yahweh." The angel is intent on changing Joshua's categories of friend and foe, ally and enemy. These categories are military and political terms; Joshua is a soldier and these are the categories he thinks and operates within. But the angel is teaching Joshua about other forms of power and uses of force, seeking to open other possibilities and actions, even perceptions of the situation to him. Yahweh fights for Israel, but battles differently than the armies of the earth. The battle plan for how Joshua is to take the city of Jericho is peculiar to say the least.

The inhabitants of Jericho had closed the city and fastened their bolts so that the Israelites could not enter. No one came in and no one went out. But on Yahweh's orders Joshua's army circles the city with the Ark, sounding trumpets to announce the Jubilee—the coming of justice—and shouting. And the walls of Jericho fall! The outcome is not a sign of Joshua's power, but of God's; the battle is not fought with the usual means. There are other ways to do battle in behalf of Yahweh. The outcome of the battle is that Joshua proclaims the city of Jericho anathema, cursed, and all that is in it is destroyed. This is the decision of Joshua, the military commander, who sacrifices the city to Yahweh.

The Angel of Yahweh comes again when the Israelites are somewhat settled in the land, during the time of the judges. It was an awkward time, full of disobedience, mistrust and misunderstandings as Israel was a loosely knit group of warring tribes with competing factions and holdings. God raised up judges to lead the people and gather them together.

The Angel of Yahweh came and sat under the sacred tree at Ophrah, which belonged to Joash, of the family of Abiezer. Gideon, the son of Joash, was threshing the wheat in a winepress to hide it from the Midianites.
The Angel of Yahweh said to him, "Yahweh be with you,

valiant warrior." Gideon answered, "Please, my lord, if
Yahweh is with us, why is all this happening to us? Where are
the wonders which our fathers recounted to us? Did they not
say that Yahweh led them up from Egypt? Why has he aban-
doned us now and given us into the hands of the Midianites?"

Yahweh then turned to him and said, "Go, and with your
courage, save Israel from the Midianites. It is I who send
you." Gideon answered: "Pardon me, Lord, but how can I
save Israel? My family is the lowliest in my tribe and I am the
least in the family of my father."

Yahweh said to him, "I will be with you and you shall
defeat the people of Midian with one single stroke." Gideon
said to him, "Please give me a sign that it is indeed you who
speak. Do not leave until I return to you with an offering and
present it to you." Yahweh responded, "I am going to wait for
you here."

Gideon went and prepared a young goat, took a measure
of flour and baked unleavened bread. He put the broth in a
pot and the meat in a basket, and went to present them to the
Angel under the tree. Then the Angel of God said to him,
"Take the meat and the bread; put them on this rock, and
pour the broth over them." Gideon did so. At that moment,
the Angel of Yahweh extended the staff he was holding and
touched the meat and the bread. Suddenly, fire blazed from
the rock. The fire consumed the meat and the bread, and the
Angel of Yahweh disappeared.

Gideon realized that he was the Angel of Yahweh and said,
"Alas, O Lord Yahweh! I have seen the Angel of Yahweh face
to face." But Yahweh said to him, "Peace be with you. Do not
fear for you shall not die." Gideon built an altar to Yahweh in
that place and called it Yahweh-Peace. To this day, it is still in
Ophrah of Abiezer. (Judg. 6:11–24)

Once again, it is the Angel of Yahweh who lures the one to be
sent on behalf of God to the place where the voice and words of

Yahweh God can be heard. And again there is the symbol of fire, which reveals the presence of God. Gideon is of the tribe of Manassah, the least of the tribes, and he's the least in the family. He is a farmer trying to survive in the midst of raids, wars, stealing and destruction. The Angel of Yahweh sets up Gideon for the task that God wants of him. He appears as a man with a staff. He meets Gideon under a sacred tree. Gideon then receives dreams that command him to destroy his father's altars to Baal and he obeys, at night because he is afraid. Then the townspeople come after him expecting Joash, Gideon's father, to hand him over, but he refuses. Battle is engaged. Gideon gathers the tribes and rallies them together to go out and meet the approaching force, and Gideon is clothed with the spirit and strength of God. Gideon approaches God and sets up another test, to assure himself that God is with him, that God is using him to save Israel by his own hand.

Then it is time to choose the army that will fight with Gideon, and now it is Yahweh God who devises the test for choosing those most suitable. God wants a small army so that the Israelites will not begin to think that they did this by their own might and power. He tells Gideon to summon the troops and tell anyone who is afraid to go home. Twenty-two thousand men return home, and Gideon has ten thousand left. Still too many, according to God. The next test is at the water's edge. They are divided into two camps: those who lap the water like a dog, and those who kneel down to drink on the other side. Only three hundred lap the water like dogs and these are the ones Yahweh God chooses for his army. All the rest go home.

The battle is bizarre. Gideon tells all the men to do what he does. Each has a jar with a torch inside in one hand and a trumpet in the other. Gideon takes one-third of the men and approaches the camp during the changing of the watch. He blows the trumpet, and all his troops smash their jars and blow their trumpets. They shout, "For Yahweh and Gideon!" The Midianites scatter as the Israelites shout and blow their horns. Gideon's soldiers do no killing; the

Midianites kill one another. Eventually people come to Gideon asking him to be their king. But Gideon answers: "I will not rule over Israel, nor my son, for Yahweh is our king" (Judg. 8:23).

Gideon's heart is in the right place, but he falls too. He takes booty from each of the soldiers—earrings of gold that all of them wore—to make an idol. Soon people from all over Israel came to that place to worship the idol, and they turned away from Yahweh. Thus Gideon too fell into the trap of his ancestors. But the story says the Midianites were so humbled that peace reigned for forty years during Gideon's lifetime. Afterward, the people no longer remembered what Yahweh had done for the people using Gideon's hand. They even stopped being grateful to Gideon's family (Judg. 8:22–35).

The story tries to remind Israel, even in the barbaric time of the judges, that God fights with the strength of the least and the weakest, not with might and strategies to be admired by generals and nations. God uses oddly chosen soldiers and the blowing of horns and torches of fire and the breaking of pots. Yahweh God is trying to teach the people what Michael learned in heaven: one must fight using the strength of God in the least likely places and people, not using military might and the power of the sword. That kind of fighting always leads to spoils of war, idolatry and unfaithfulness—forgetfulness of God and ingratitude.

This kind of fighting is understood by the poor and those who still struggle for justice. In Nicaragua the story is told of women who did battle in front of the church, clanging their pots and pans together and singing hymns of praise and cries of freedom and hope against the armed soldiers of Somoza the dictator. On that day the women were slaughtered, but it was the turning point in the struggle for freedom. The courage of the women and the brutal response spurred the nation to rally and stand as one against the violence and indiscriminate killing of the innocent.

This Angel of Yahweh, Michael the archangel, is often made the patron and protector of dioceses that experience persecution, torture, suffering and death at the hands of those who use violence, "disappearances" and lies against those who seek to honor God and follow Jesus' nonviolent resistance to evil. Oscar Romero, the bishop of San Salvador, called on Michael the archangel as the defender of his diocese and people in their struggle for life. He proclaimed that San Miguel Archangel fights on their behalf and stands with them. His presence was and is summoned to defend all the sanctuaries, temples, churches and cathedrals of the land and all the people who gather there to praise God in the midst of violence and death. It is Michael, Romero said, who stands at the entrances to the churches and before their altars as guardian and protector of God's own servants.

> We believe in what is seen and unseen and so rely on the presence of God's angels to express and live out our faith. It is Michael who, with his great censor of smoking fire, offers to God all the supplications, prayers, works, sufferings and hopes of all the people and who defends us from danger and evil. Michael serves only God and bends to Jesus Christ and all who serve him. He has fought and stays with those who struggle to be faithful until once again all things will be subject to Jesus Christ, the Lamb of God whose blood is testimony to our life. We are protected from the dragon and all that would seek to harm us—of this we are assured (Romero, freely translated).

And so Michael, the defender of the people of God, has come to be associated with churches, literally as a patron of church buildings and more expansively as the protector of the Church, the people of God, the presence of the risen Christ in the world. There are many enchanting legends about one church in particular: Mount St. Michael in France. It is believed that hermits and anchorites lived on the mount as early as the sixth century. Legends abound around St. Aubert, who was the builder of the church on the mount. Born in 660, he became a priest and the bishop of Avranches under strange circumstances. This is how the story goes:

- When the old bishop died, the clergy and the people gathered together to decide upon a new bishop, as was the custom. But they couldn't agree on one person, so they decided to fast for a week and pray to the Holy Spirit to show the person God wanted as their bishop. On the seventh day they assembled in the church. There they heard a great clap of thunder and a voice saying: "Aubert, my priest, will be your bishop." As the voice was heard, a flame descended on Aubert that filled the church with dazzling light. They all decided with one voice: Aubert is our bishop. Aubert didn't think to disagree!

The stories grew.

- One day, in returning to his diocese, a group of villagers surrounded Aubert and told him that a dragon attacked their flocks every day. So Aubert resolved to go and fight the dragon.

  He went after the dragon, which was breathing fire out of its nose and mouth. Everyone else fled in terror, but Aubert held his ground, unafraid. He made the sign of the cross on the dragon and threw his stole at it, commanding: "Approach not, and stir no more than if you were dead."

  The dragon stopped in its tracks, and the people slowly came back. The dragon obeyed the bishop's orders. Aubert then commanded it to harm no one ever again, including the sheep. The beast turned and fled into the sea, and the people and the bishop went to the church to thank God for deliverance.

But the best story of all regards the bishop's dream.

- Aubert gathered the people together and told them that St. Michael had appeared to him and told him to build a chapel on the Mount of the Tomb [the mount's original name] so that he might be honored there. Aubert went on to say that he was troubled—how was he supposed to know if it was really Michael? So he ignored the dream.

Days later Michael appeared again, with a rather severe look on his face, and told Aubert he wanted a chapel in that place and that he shouldn't be so slow in obeying him. Like Gideon, Aubert was concerned about really knowing who this was, and he remembered John's admonition to test the spirits. He prayed, kept vigil, fasted, did penance, and assisted the poor with greater care so that the prayers of the poor would help him decide what to do.

"I'm sure," he said to them, "you've noticed that I've been doing this for the past few weeks. Well, last night I was exhausted and finally fell asleep. Michael came again. He severely reproved me for not obeying him and he reached out and touched my forehead with his finger—the mark you can still see openly." Indeed, they could all see the hole in the bishop's head!

"Then Michael told me that I was to build the chapel in the place where a bull was tethered. It had been stolen and I was to return it to its owner and to make the church as large as the area trodden underfoot by the bull."

So Aubert and the people all climbed the mount, a three-hour trek, and found the bull just as it had been described. Nowadays the land between Avranches and Mount St. Michael is beach, a long stretch that, at certain tides, can separate the church from land. They found the bull on a long tether, and the area he had trodden covered by dew—easily marked out. Immediately Aubert blessed the spot where the sanctuary would stand.

The legends differ slightly. Some say that when Michael came the second time, he was specific in details of the church's architecture, down to precise positioning of windows, turrets, rafters, glass, sanctuary, altars, buttresses, and so on. But when Aubert awoke, he promptly forgot it all. So when Michael came again, he touched

Aubert's forehead—more like drilled a hole in his head—and put the blueprints inside safe and secure. When he awoke, Aubert found a hole in his head and remembered all the designs.

The church was built according to the angel's specifications. Everything essential was there except water. So Aubert prayed: "As in the desert water sprang from a hard stone for the thirsting people, so in thy kindness, O God, give water to the Mount which has none." Michael the archangel promptly appeared and showed Aubert a stone. When he lifted it, water sprang forth. This fountain is called St. Aubert's Fountain. A tower is built around it which projects from the ramparts of the abbey. It is dry now; the spring has dried up.

The time came for Bishop Aubert to die, causing great sorrow. He requested to be buried in the chapel of St. Michael with his head facing the altar. The poor and those in need would come to pray, for he had been so kind and generous to them. The skull still bore the hole in the forehead where Michael had touched him and made him remember how to build the church. The skull is in the Church of St. Gervase in Avranches.

The Church of Mount St. Michael is tightly linked to the history of France and Normandy. It has been burned to the ground on a number of occasions and always rebuilt. Over the years the church has been a fortress, a state prison and house of detention. It remains a symbol of the soul of France and a vision of what it can do for the glory of God. It soars into the sky as an everlasting prayer; the seas at high tide and the sands at low tide speak of the infinity of God. Sometimes it appears to be on fire as the sun sets.

This symbol of fire continues throughout devotional literature and belief. St. Francis of Assisi had great devotion to the angels. He would celebrate a "mini-Lent" beginning on the Feast of the Holy Cross, September 14, in remembrance of the passion of Jesus and the cross, concluding on the Feast of St. Michael the Archangel and All Angels on September 29. When in prayer on the mountain—

meditating on the passion of Jesus—an angel came to give him the wounds of Christ on the cross. It was Michael who came in fire to stir Francis's heart to flame and draw him into the passion of Christ. Michael, the Angel of Yahweh, is intimate with struggle, suffering and death in the face of sin and evil and with the souls and spirits of those who seek the honor of God and are known for their love and care for the poor, the victims of injustice and sin.

There is a chaplet of St. Michael that is prayed often in France. There are nine salutations to Michael and the choirs of angels, along with an Our Father and three Aves:

By the intercession of St. Michael and the celestial choir of seraphim, may the Lord make us worthy to burn with the fire of perfect charity.

By the intercession of St. Michael and the celestial choir of cherubim, may the Lord vouchsafe to grant us the grace to leave the ways of wickedness and run in the paths of Christian perfection.

By the intercession of St. Michael and the celestial choir of thrones, may the Lord infuse into our hearts a true and sincere spirit of humility.

By the intercession of Michael and the celestial choir of dominions, may the Lord give us grace to govern our senses and subdue our unruly passions.

By the intercession of St. Michael and the celestial choir of powers, may the Lord vouchsafe to protect our souls against the snares and temptations of the devil.

By the intercession of St. Michael and the celestial choir of virtues, may the Lord preserve us from evil and suffer us not to fall into temptation.

By the intercession of St. Michael and the celestial choir of principalities, may God fill our souls with a true spirit of obedience.

By the intercession of St. Michael and the celestial choir of archangels, may the Lord give us perseverance in faith and all good works, in order that we gain the glory of paradise. By the intercession of St. Michael and the celestial choir of angels, may the Lord grant us to be protected by them in this mortal life and conducted hereafter to eternal glory. Amen.

Angels. These creatures of light share the same domain with us and are intricately intertwined with the history and the salvation of human beings in the plan of God. We work together or we work in opposition to the mysterious unfolding of creation and blessing. We all choose: angelic spirit and human being alike. What will we choose?

2

GABRIEL

Archangel of Truth

The Jewish sages tell a story about the creation of human beings. It tells of a conversation between God and the angels about whether Adam and Eve and all their descendants should be created. It is a piece of all our story.

- Once upon a time, when God was about to create Adam out of clay from the ground and breathe his own breath into his mouth, kissing him with his own life, he called all the attending angels that he had made before him. And they assembled, tier upon tier, rank upon rank, from the cherubim to the lowly angels. God told them of his intent and asked them what they thought of the idea. There was much discussion and much dissension in the ranks. Some said: Yes, of course, create them. And others were just as sure: No, no, you will regret it. Do not create them.

  Some cried out: Remember the words that will be spoken and sung in praise of you, O God. "Grace and truth shall be met and justice and peace embraced." The Angel of Justice said: God, create them, for they will learn to live justly and to practice charity. But the Angel of Peace spoke against, saying: Lord, do not create them, for they will just fight and quarrel and seek to destroy one another and all that you have so loved and made. Then the Angel of Grace spoke on their behalf, saying: Remember, O God, your mercy and create them, for they will imitate you in acts of kindness and tender care. And the Angel of Truth spoke last and most forcibly: O God, do not create them. You know all that is to come to pass. They will lie and defraud and be deceitful, without integrity, and will even use your name to validate their dishonesty.

God, blessed be his name, listened to them all and, in response, grasped the Angel of Truth and cast her down to the earth. The angels were stunned and in grief and surprise cried out: O God, do you despise the Angel of Truth, who is your seal and source of words so much that you would exile her and cast her forth from your presence? In your goodness, regret your word and let her rise again from the earth! Remember, it is written: "And Truth rises from the earth."

The sages say that it is up to us, created by the Holy One, to lift up Truth and let her rise from the earth to the heavens and to once again be in the presence of God. This is what God expects of us: to be holy unto God, to be truthful, living with integrity and so to honor God in word, in action and deed, in liturgy and in manner of life. Truth is given to us to return home to God, blessed be his name.

The Angel of Truth, messenger of God, deliverer of good news, announcer of God breaking into history and altering the destinies of individuals and of peoples, of the whole human race, is traditionally called Gabriel. This Angel of God is best known for his visit to Myriam, betrothed to Joseph of the house of David, summoning all of history to the moment of annunciation: the advent of the long-awaited One into the world. But Gabriel already had a long history before he appeared before the maidservant of God, Mary of Nazareth. Mary, as a devoted Jew, heir to the Torah and the scriptures of the Jewish community, undoubtedly associated all of those accounts and stories of Gabriel with her own visitation.

Gabriel appears first, named specifically, in the Book of Daniel. The Book of Daniel is not daily reading for many Christians, and yet it contains crucial seeds of the promise of covenant—visions, dreams and teachings on how to live truthfully as believers in a world that is antagonistic to belief. The world is dangerous and fraught with destruction and persecution for those who call themselves servants of the Holy One and seek to obey and make decisions with integrity.

At the time of Daniel, the people and nation of Israel were dealing with cataclysmic changes that came to be reflected in the beliefs, prayer and practices of the Jewish people. The Book of Daniel, telling the story of the Jewish exile in Babylon, was written from the vantage point of the time of Nebuchadnezzar of Babylon and Cyrus of Persia, looking ahead to the horrible events that the Jews would experience under Antiochus. Daniel is a prophet of announcement, foretelling future hard events and issuing the call to be steadfast, courageous and faithful in the face of such evil.

The book begins with Daniel, who is from a royal family in Israel, being taken as a slave into the court of Nebuchadnezzar and trained in the languages and literature of the court. After three years he would take a place in the king's service.

Daniel and three of his friends rise to high positions. Then the king has a statue erected in the plain of Dura and orders everyone to worship it. Anyone who refuses will be thrown into a burning furnace. Daniel's three friends refuse to obey, of course. Bound fast, they are hurled into the furnace. The furnace is so hot that even the men who throw them into the fire are burned to death. But the three Israelites walked in the midst of the flames, singing to God and praising the Lord. The king's servants keep feeding the fire, searing even onlookers as the flames mount.

And then an angel appears with the three men.

But the angel of the Lord came down into the furnace beside Azariah and his companions; he drove the flames of the fire outside the furnace, and blew upon them, in the middle of the furnace, a coolness like that of wind and dew, so that the fire did not touch them or cause them pain or trouble them. (Dan. 3:49–50)

The king sees *four* men walking around in the furnace and declares that one of them looks like a son of the gods—common parlance for angels in the ancient nations and times. The king orders the three, whom he now calls the servants of the Most High God, to come out and they do so. Then the king prays publicly:

"Blessed be the God of Shadrach, Meshach and Abednego, who sent his angel to free his servants who, trusting in him, disobeyed the king's order and preferred to give their bodies to the fire rather than serve and worship any other god but their God." (Dan. 3:95)

The king decrees that no one from any race, nation or language may speak irreverently of this God, who is God like no other.

Later Darius the Mede takes over the kingdom, while Daniel keeps ascending in power. Darius decrees that anyone who worships or prays to any god other than the king himself is to be thrown into a lions' den. Daniel is quickly betrayed and brought before the king, who tells him: "May your God, whom you serve faithfully, save you." Daniel is thrown to the lions and a stone is put at the mouth of the den. The next morning the king comes back after a sleepless night to see what has happened to Daniel:

As he came near he called in an anguished voice, "Daniel, servant of the living God, did your God whom you serve faithfully save you from the lions?"

Daniel answered: "Live forever, O king! My God sent his angel who closed the lions' mouths so that they did not hurt me. God did that because I am innocent in his sight. Neither have I wronged you, O king." (Dan. 6:20–22)

Daniel is released and those who accused him are fed to the lions. Being very hungry, they tear them to pieces and feast on them quickly. Then King Darius decrees and writes to the nations of Daniel's God, "who is the living God and forever he endures; his kingdom will not be crushed, his dominion will never cease."

These stories are the prelude to all that follows. Daniel's life symbolizes the life of the Israelite community, the nation that belongs to God. His prophetic obedience, truthfulness and faithfulness, when imitated, will result in all the nations seeing the glory of God revealed in the outcome of history and the rise of the Jewish people, who are protected by God who orders all history. One day, all nations will see the glory of this God who is the God of life, whose kingdom cannot be crushed and whose dominion is forever.

Daniel then begins to have his visions of the future—the terrifying future that the Jews will know under the tyrant Antiochus IV of Syria. These visions are intended to encourage the people to see that history serves the God of life and to see themselves as servants of this God, like Daniel, teaching the nations by obedience, integrity and enduring courage in the face of persecution and death.

Daniel's visions continue, specifically about the "Abomination of the devastator" who "put Abomination in place of the sacrifice and flung Truth to the ground. And whatever it undertook succeeded" (Dan. 8:12). And now Gabriel appears:

> As I, Daniel, looked at this vision and tried to understand it, I suddenly saw before me someone like a man, and I heard a human voice over the river Ulai that cried out to him: "Gabriel, explain the vision to this man."
>
> He approached the place where I was. When he came, I was terrified and fell on my face. He said to me, "Son of man, understand: this vision refers to the end-time." As he spoke, I lost consciousness and fell face down on the ground. He touched me and raised me to my feet. Then he said, "See, I

will reveal to you what is going to happen, when the wrath comes to an end, for the end is set." (Dan. 8:15–19)

Gabriel enters the world and human affairs. He enters as one who reveals the future, as one who touches the prophet and raises him up on his feet to see the vision of wrath, and he enters as one who is dedicated to the Truth—the end is set. Gabriel enters as one who explains, who interprets dreams to one who has already the gift of interpretation. This encounter with Gabriel leaves Daniel frightened because of the vision and its contents and his own lack of understanding.

Gabriel's words of explanation make Daniel faint; he is sick to his stomach for several days. So Daniel pleads with God in prayer and fasting, doing penance, putting on sack cloth and sitting on an ash pile. His prayer is ardent, on behalf of the people who are sinners, with Daniel including himself among them. It is a resume of the past and present events, seen in response to the justice of God, who is right to punish the people for breaking the covenant and insulting the honor of God. And yet, Daniel prays for mercy and pardon for the people, even though they have not sought to calm Yahweh's anger or do homage or obey God's laws and decrees. He prays: "Listen, Lord! Lord, forgive! Pay attention to us, Lord! Act, my God, and do not delay for your own sake, since your city and your people are called by your name" (Dan. 9:19).

And in the midst of his prayer, Gabriel comes again, flying:

At the hour of the evening sacrifice, I was still speaking, confessing my sins and those of Israel, my people, begging Yahweh on behalf of his Holy Mountain.

At that moment, Gabriel, whom I had seen at the beginning of the vision, came to me, flying, and he said to me, "Daniel, I have come now to make you understand. As you were praying, a word was uttered and I have come to teach it to you because

God loves you. Pay attention to this word and understand the vision.

"Seventy weeks are set for your people and your holy city, to put an end to transgression, to put sin under lock, to wipe out the offense, and to bring everlasting justice, so that the visions and the prophecies will be fulfilled and the Holy of Holies be anointed." (Dan. 9:20–24)

Gabriel has just announced the coming of the kingdom of God! But it is the introduction to it that is remarkable. Gabriel comes in response to Daniel's prayer during the time of the evening sacrifice and comes to make him understand and teach him the word that was uttered because God loves him. This is prelude to the annunciation that Mary hears, the announcement of the coming of the One who will care for the holy ones of God. The explanation goes on in detail, in symbolic and enigmatic sayings that describe history from another vantage point, that of divine intervention and peace that is set, that is decided already.

Gabriel is sent to reveal the truth and to bring strength to the weak and those who have trouble facing the truth in the midst of suffering and death. Gabriel brings peace and tells Daniel "not to fear" but to have "courage and be strong" so that he can face the truth and what lies ahead. Then Daniel can serve God in history and work with Gabriel and Michael who are his guardian angels, the guardian angels of the holy ones, the people of God on earth, caught in history and struggling against Persia and Greece and all those nations that stand in opposition to the coming of the kingdom of God. This is the announcement of the Messiah, the vision of hope that will sustain the people through long generations.

In chapter 12 the vision brings more hope of fulfillment and more angels.

At that time, Michael will rise, the Great Commander who defends the sons of your people. It shall be a time of anguish as never before since the nations first existed until this very day.

Then all those whose names are written in the Book will be saved....

I, Daniel, looked and saw two others standing, one on either side of the river. One said to the man clothed in linen who was upstream, "When will these wonderful things take place?" And I heard the answer of the man in linen who was upstream. He raised his hands to heaven and swore by the One who lives eternally: "Everything will be fulfilled within a time, two times and a half a time. When the holy people is completely crushed and without any strength, then these things will be fulfilled." (Dan. 12:1, 5–7)

These visions are complex and perplexing. They are about the end of time, the end of the ages, the end of nations, the end of rulers, the end of the rise of certain powers on earth, the end of belief and experience as any group knows them and feels secure in them. The visions are constant in revealing and reminding the earth that God rules history and all the nations whether they know that they serve him or not. In the end, truth will rise again and be known and honored. Persecution will end and vindication will come to faithful individuals and those who live with integrity. Those who do evil understand nothing and evil does abound, but it will one day end and all will be held accountable and rewarded or condemned publicly. The times and dates are not known. Like Daniel, we are to go our way and wait until the end, trusting in God's justice. God's promises are set and truth will prevail. Gabriel brings truth to the earth, reveals and interprets it and reminds those who are faithful and intent on true wisdom that God is with them no matter what transpires in the world. This is the pattern of Gabriel's meetings with those of earth.

Traditionally in the Jewish and Christian communities it is the archangel Gabriel who also visits a number of individuals important to the life and future of the Jewish community: Hagar; Jacob; the wife of Manoah, who is the mother of Samson; Zechariah, priest and husband of Elizabeth, father of John the Baptizer; Mary and Joseph; the magi; and the shepherds.

In the Book of Genesis, Hagar, the slave woman of Sarai given to Abram to conceive a child, is the first woman to encounter this angel, traditionally Gabriel, who visits Abram also. Hagar, the black slave purchased in Egypt, has been treated so badly by Sarai that she runs away, believing it better to die in the desert than to live under such oppression in Sarai's house. Hagar is in dire straits, caught in the desert without water and without hope for a future life for herself and her child, when she encounters Gabriel.

> The angel of Yahweh found her near a spring in the wilderness and said to her, "Hagar, servant of Sarai, where have you come from and where are you going?" She said, "I'm running away from Sarai, my mistress." The angel of Yahweh said to her, "Go back to your mistress and humbly submit yourself to her." The angel of Yahweh said to her, "I will so increase your descendants, that they will be too numerous to be counted." Then the angel of Yahweh said to her, "Now you are with child and you will have a son, and you shall name him Ishmael, for Yahweh has heard your distress. He shall be a wild ass of a man, his hand against everyone and everyone's hand against him, defiant towards all his brothers."
>
> Hagar gave to Yahweh who spoke to her the name of El Roi, for she said: "I have seen the One who sees me." That is why this well is called the well of Lahai-roi. It is between Kadesh and Bered.
>
> Hagar gave birth to a son and Abram called the child Hagar bore him Ishmael. Abram was eighty-six years old when Hagar gave birth to Ishmael. (Gen. 16:7–15)

The angel asks about Hagar's past and future. He questions her and gives her the promise of a future not only for her child, but for a people so numerous that they cannot be counted.

Traditionally, in the Muslim community, Hagar is the mother of Islam and her children are the followers of Mohammed. She is told that Yahweh has paid heed to her sufferings and heard her cry of despair and will bless her. The angel tells her to return to her bondage, to endure with gracefulness, knowing that Yahweh is with her and her offspring. Hagar obeys the angel, knowing that her future is more life-giving than her present slavery. She prays to Yahweh and names the place of the angel, that well that promised life, "God sees." The angel encourages and yet commands obedience in one who was vengeful and humiliated. But now Hagar is free. She knows God and knows that God is the God of the living, who sees all of history. She can return, knowing she and her son and their descendants will know God and be seen and known. All the earth is God's.

Once again Hagar must run from Sarah and Abraham, who are now intent on killing her and her child, who is growing up and seen as competition and problematic to Sarah's future. Again, Hagar, now with Ishmael, heads out into the desert. They soon run out of water and reach a dead end. The angel comes again.

> As she sat there, the child began to wail. God heard him and the angel of God called to Hagar from heaven and said, "What is the matter, Hagar? Don't be afraid. God has heard the boy crying. Get up, pick the boy up and hold him safely, for I will make him into a great nation." God then opened her eyes and she saw a well of water. She went and filled the skin and gave the boy a drink. (Gen. 21:16b–19)

Gabriel is sent again to save Hagar from death, to give water and hope, and to proclaim a future for a people and the presence of God with that people. Hagar twice sees the angel Gabriel and knows the proclamation of a coming kingdom and a lasting life and hope for a people founded by God, who is with her and her son and their people. This angel is about visions and about children who make visions and unbounded hopes come true in time.

Later, Gabriel again appears in human history.

Jacob, the younger son of Isaac, steals his brother's birthright and blessing and flees home. He works for Laban for seven years for the woman he loves, Rachel, but Laban deceives him and gives him Leah, her older sister, instead. He must work seven years more for Rachel. Eventually he has eleven sons and a daughter (his twelfth and youngest son, Benjamin, will be born later near Bethlehem), and he has prospered greatly.

When he decides to return to his home in Canaan, he hears that his estranged brother Esau is coming to meet him with four hundred men. Jacob thinks that he is coming to attack him and get even with him after all these years for stealing his father's blessing and Esau's birthright. Jacob has already left Laban's camp and as he goes on his way he meets some angels of God. "On seeing them Jacob exclaimed, 'This is God's camp,' and he named the place Mahanaim" (Gen. 32:3). He continues and grows more fearful that Esau is coming after him. He sends servants with gifts and messages that he is coming and describes himself as Esau's servant…. That night Jacob takes Rachel and Leah and his sons and maidservants and crosses the Jabbok at the ford, leaving them on one side and he alone on the other side.

Then a man wrestled with him until daybreak. When the man saw that he could not get the better of Jacob, he struck him in the socket of his hip and dislocated it as he wrestled with him.

The man said, "Let me go, for day is breaking." But Jacob said, "I will not let you go until you have given me your blessing." The man then said, "What is your name?" "Jacob" was the reply. He answered, "You will no longer be called Jacob, but Israel, for you have been strong-with-God as you have been with men and have prevailed."

Then Jacob asked him, "What is your name?" He

answered: "Why do you ask my name?" And he blessed him there. So Jacob called the place Peniel, saying, "I have seen God face to face and survived." The sun rose as he passed through Peniel, limping because of his hip. (Gen. 32:24–31)

Jacob wrestles with the angel all night and neither one can win or subdue the other, though the angel dislocates Jacob's hip, making him limp the rest of his days. But Jacob leaves with his blessing and a new name—Israel. Jacob, which means "trickster" or "activist," describes what he has often done in the past. But now and for the future he is Israel, "strong with God." He clings to the angel for a blessing, for a dearer life and a truer life, and he is given what he seeks.

Praying is struggling for truth, for justice, for goodness, in us and in the world. Prayer is about restoring what has been stolen and giving gifts. It is about becoming a servant, asking forgiveness of those we have wronged. It is about reconstituting relationships, making whole the community, serving truth. It leaves its mark on us. We are scared, limping. We remember our sin and forgiveness and our need to heal what we have destroyed. Prayer is a way of living, a journey that is never ended, but lived in the presence of God at certain moments, especially moments of truth, reconciliation and justice.

In this story, as in many of the stories of the Hebrew scriptures, the Angel of Yahweh is hard to distinguish from Yahweh's presence itself. Sometimes people experience God's angel and sometimes it appears to be an experience of God. They overlap and are blurred together. Often the stories begin with an angel of God that brings someone into the presence of God to hear the voice or word of God. What is seen is the angel; the One to be obeyed, however, is Yahweh. The angel is God's presence attentive to human beings' needs and place and future. The angel reveals God's intent and designs in these situations and circumstances. The moments are one time, unrepeatable, momentarily a reality. Then the angels and the presence disappear.

When Jacob dies, he blesses Joseph and says:

"May the God in whose presence my fathers Abraham and Isaac walked, the God who has been my shepherd from my birth to this day, the Angel who has saved me from every evil, bless these boys. And in them may my name live on and that of my fathers Abraham and Isaac. And may they increase greatly on the earth!" (Gen. 48:15–16)

Jacob is no longer a "hanger-on." He has wrestled with power and claimed its blessing—his rightful one, not stolen this time but wrested from life and experience, from the knowledge of God, suffering, forgiveness and reconciliation. Israel will be the descendants of Jacob, Leah and Rachel—they will be the ones who are strong with God when they are true to their calling and their identity as the children of Yahweh. The angels, especially Gabriel, will call them back to this truth again and again throughout history. All of history seems wrapped up in their experiences of God and angels.

This angel comes again in the book of Judges to the wife of Manoah, a man of Zorah of the tribe of Dan. The story has many familiar characteristics: one who will belong to God and serve the people, and yet, with weaknesses and sin, be a part of the ensuing history and suffering of the people as well.

There was a man of Zorah of the tribe of Dan, called Manoah. His wife could not bear children. The Angel of Yahweh appeared to this woman and said to her, "You have not borne children and have not given birth, but see, you are to conceive and give birth to a son. Because of this, take care not to take wine or any alcoholic drink, or eat unclean foods from now on, for you shall bear a son who shall be a Nazirite of Yahweh from the womb of his mother. Never shall his hair be cut for he is consecrated to Yahweh. He shall begin the liberation of the Israelites from the Philistine oppression." (Judg. 13:2–5)

The stage is set. A barren couple, a time of bondage. The woman receives a visit from an angel who announces that her child will be the hope and future of the present times and part of the liberation of Israel. She is commanded to do certain things to consecrate her child to the Lord, even while in her womb.

The woman tells her husband about the angel, and her husband prays to God about how to bring up the child. However, the angel comes again to the woman out in the fields, and this time she runs and gets her husband who questions the man/angel: "When your word is fulfilled, what rule and direction shall the boy follow?" But the angel speaks only of what the woman must do, repeating that she must do all that the angel commanded her. Then Manoah says to the Angel of Yahweh: "Permit us to detain you and prepare a young goat for you." (Manoah did not know that the man was the Angel of Yahweh). That small aside is crucial. His wife has told him and the angel has spoken to him, and still he doesn't know whom he is speaking with and who is before him! The angel is blunt. "Even if I did stay, I would not taste your food. But if you want to offer a burnt offering, offer it to Yahweh" (Judg. 13:16). Always the focus is on Yahweh and the true worship and who is to be honored and served; it is never the angel, only the One the angel represents and obeys. Manoah persists with his questions. He wants to know the angel's name and, as usual, the angel says: "Why do you ask my name?... It is Wonderful." Then Manoah offers the holocaust to Yahweh who does wonderful things. And as Manoah and his wife look on, a fire breaks forth from the altar rising toward heaven and the Angel of Yahweh ascends in the flame (Judg. 13:20). They fall on their faces and finally Manoah knows that the man is the Angel of Yahweh. He tells his wife that they will surely die because they have seen the Angel of God, and the woman, much more understanding of all that has happened, says to him:

"If Yahweh had wanted to kill us, he would not have accepted the holocaust or the offering from our hand; he would not have made all these things happen or said what we have just heard." The woman gave birth to a son and named him Samson. The boy grew and Yahweh blessed him. Then the Spirit of Yahweh began to move him when he was in Mahane Dan between Zorah and Eshtaol. (Judg. 13:23–25)

These two women who saw angels, Hagar and Manoah's wife, are intimately connected to the future of Israel in their children, their sons, whom the Spirit of God claims and leads into the future. With Manoah's wife, the child will be a liberator. What the women do in response to the angels to make the future a reality—often bearing hardship and enduring oppression—is crucial so that others may know the freedom and liberation that they hope for. The men often struggle, wrestle and reevaluate the meanings of violence and power; the women must endure and give birth to hope. Both must alter their thoughts and experiences of reality to see differently, to look into the future with the eyes of the angels of Yahweh.

These stories all come to fulfillment in most surprising ways when Gabriel comes into Mary's presence in Nazareth, bringing together many of these disparate pieces to make an announcement that is unbelievable. The story begins with Zechariah, the priest of the family of Aaron, married to Elizabeth, who cannot have children. Barrenness is unbearably painful and humiliating for the wife of any Jew, but especially so for the wife of a priest. The angel comes to Zechariah in the temple while he is fulfilling his office with others. The description of Zechariah and Elizabeth is important:

In the days of Herod, king of Judea, there lived a priest named Zechariah, belonging to the priestly clan of Abiah. Elizabeth, Zechariah's wife, also belonged to a priestly family. Both of them were upright in the eyes of God and lived blamelessly in accordance with all the laws and commands of the Lord, but they had no child. Elizabeth could not have any and now they were both very old. (Luke 1:5–7)

The stories with angels are always located precisely in history. The people who are visited are described in the eyes of God as faithful, obedient and true. This is the opening of the door, the entering of the angel into history. This is intervention, interruption and God's presence moving in individual lives on behalf of all the people. It is always momentous and it is most often hidden, known only to a few, the poor and the righteous. The beginnings are shrouded in mystery, veiled by wings and buried in deeper truths that are not easily seen or understood by those who are not faithful. They come to those already expectant and living on the word of the Lord, hoping for deliverance and liberation.

When Zechariah enters the sanctuary of the Lord to burn incense, the people are gathered outside (at the evening service perhaps, as in the book of Daniel). The story is familiar and full of allusions.

An angel of the Lord appeared to him, standing on the right side of the altar of incense. On seeing the angel, Zechariah was deeply troubled and fear took hold of him.

But the angel said to him, "Don't be afraid, Zechariah, be assured that your prayer has been heard. Your wife Elizabeth will bear you a son and you shall name him John. He will bring joy and gladness to you, and many will rejoice at his birth.

"This son of yours will be great in the eyes of the Lord. Listen: he shall never drink wine or strong drink; but he will be filled with the Holy Spirit even from his mother's womb. Through him many of the people of Israel will turn to the Lord their God. He himself will open the way to the Lord with the spirit and power of the prophet Elijah; he will reconcile fathers and children, and lead the disobedient to wisdom and righteousness, in order to make ready for the Lord a people prepared."

Zechariah said to the angel: "How can I believe such a thing? I am an old man and my wife is elderly too." The angel replied: "I am Gabriel, who stands before God, and I am the one sent to speak to you and bring you this good news! My words will come true in their time, although you would not believe. But now you will be silent and unable to speak until this has happened." (Luke 1:11–20)

The elements of many of the other stories are also in this one. Elizabeth, like so many of the matriarchs of Israel, cannot bear children. They do so only by the power of God in the covenant, not in the usual ways. The pattern continues—the kindness of God takes note of them and answers their prayers and lifts the curse of childlessness that others see them living under. God gives them hope for a future life and remembrance among the people. Elizabeth is like Sarah and Hagar, Rebecca, Rachel, Hannah and the wife of Manoah, humbled by lack and powerlessness, blessed by Yahweh.

The angel begins by calming Zechariah's fears and then gives an announcement of joy, gladness and hope. Though what is to come has no basis in fact now, it will be wonderful to behold. It is the work of God. All the talk is of the child to come—who he is, what he will do for the people and how he will serve God's ends. This child who lives in the eyes of God is named from the womb. This child has spirit from his mother's womb and will never drink of any spirit but the spirit that possessed Elijah and the prophets. His power is to reconcile the generations, to convert the disobedient to wisdom and righteousness and to prepare a whole people for the Lord's ways and designs. His birth will bring joy and gladness to many (those who are faithful and waiting on the promises of God), and he will set in motion even more wondrous things.

But Zechariah is dubious. He tells the angel he doesn't believe the word, doesn't believe that much in the power of God. He's old and so is his wife; there's little hope for them.

The angel responds by identifying himself as Gabriel, the one who came to Daniel, the one who gives courage and explains the events of the future truthfully. He is clear that his words will become reality whether Zechariah believes them or not. Refusing to believe in the good news, refusing to believe in God's power will rob Zechariah temporarily of the voice that was so quick to rebuke and refuse the presence of God wanting to be made known in words and history. Zechariah is struck dumb, and the time of mercy for Elizabeth begins. Indeed Elizabeth marvels, praising God: "What is the Lord doing for me! This is his time for mercy and for taking away my public disgrace" (Luke 1:25).

The time is fulfilled, and Elizabeth gives birth to a son. On the eighth day the circumcision rite and naming ceremony are to be celebrated, consecrating the firstborn to the Lord in remembrance of the binding of Isaac. The family and neighbors want to name him Zechariah after his father, but his mother speaks up boldly:

> "Not so; he shall be called John." They said to her, "No one in your family has that name"; and they asked the father by means of signs for the name he wanted to give. Zechariah asked for a writing table and wrote on it "His name is John," and they were very surprised. Immediately Zechariah could speak again and his first words were in praise of God. A holy fear came on all in the neighborhood, and throughout the Hills of Judah the people talked about these events. As they heard this, they pondered in their minds and wondered, "What will this child be?" For they understood that the hand of the Lord was with him. (Luke 1:60–66)

In acknowledging the truth—"His name is John"—Zechariah gives testimony to the angel Gabriel's announcement of the truth of this child and the future of Israel. In writing the truth his tongue is loosed and he is free to speak. His first words are praise and blessing of God. Zechariah is filled with the Holy Spirit and sings the canticle we now call the Benedictus. He tells the truth of the past, what God has done for the people and how God always is true to the divine word and holy covenant. Zechariah speaks of the effect of the truthfulness of God's word: we become a holy and righteous people to serve God all the days of our lives. Then he turns to his child—the child that belongs to God from his mother's womb—and tells the people what the angel announced to him: who this child is and what God will do for Israel in this child. John will prepare God's way, leading the people to salvation. And all this is the work of God, the expression of God's mercy, which comes as "a rising sun shining on those who live in darkness and in the shadow of death, and guiding our feet into the way of peace." Truth grows stronger, appears more openly, and the way opens before the One who is the Way, the Truth and the Light. In the Eastern churches, this John is himself an angel who goes before the face of Jesus, who is human and divine, who is the union of creation. As it was in the beginning is now and will be forever.

Three months before John's naming, the angel Gabriel comes again to Israel to a town of Galilee called Nazareth. He approaches a young woman engaged to Joseph of the family of David. Her name is Mary. The setting is humble, out of the way, off the beaten path, a small town, but here history will be altered forever—if the woman believes the truth of God's promises and ever-reliable word.

> The angel came to her and said, "Rejoice, full of grace, the Lord is with you." Mary listened and was troubled at these words, wondering what this greeting could mean. (Luke 1:28–29)

Mary's reaction is much like the prophet Daniel's response to seeing Gabriel. There is a sense of upset, of dislocation, of weakness, of things to come beyond human control and power; of earth-shattering events that serve the mysterious plan of God, and God's intervention in the lives of the people of Israel.

And so the angel speaks with reassurance, as Gabriel did with Daniel:

"Do not fear, Mary, for God has looked kindly on you. You shall conceive and bear a son and you shall call him Jesus. He will be great and shall rightly be called Son of the Most High. The Lord God will give him the kingdom of David, his ancestor; he will rule over the people of Jacob forever and his reign shall have no end." (Luke 1:30–33)

Mary listens, absorbs the message and asks, "How can this be if I am a virgin?" She knows her own reality. She also senses the magnitude of what will happen from the child's names: Jesus—Savior, Joshua, Son of the Most High. She knows that this child is the future of her people, of Israel for all time, without end. She is not disbelieving but expectant, opening a door for unseen reality and unthought-of possibility. And the angel answers:

"The Holy Spirit will come upon you and the power of the Most High will overshadow you; therefore, the holy child to be born shall be called Son of God. Even your relative Elizabeth is expecting a son in her old age, although she was unable to have a child, and she is now in her sixth month. With God nothing is impossible." (Luke 1:35–37)

The reply is full of mystery, of unknowns, of future experiences that will defy the natural order of creation; this is a seismic shift in history, something up to this point unimaginable. "The Holy Spirit will overshadow you." This echoes the tradition of prophets and kings and mountains where God dwelled and visited, on Sinai and in the Temple itself, where the Ark of the Covenant was kept in the sanctuary, the Holy of Holies. The power of God, as all the angelic stories of the Hebrew scriptures have tried to reveal, is nothing like power in the world. The power of God bends and breaks all boundaries and shatters all preconceptions. It does the impossible easily as it plays with creation's order and seeds earth and believers with hope and life and grace.

Mary's response is most remarkable, most graceful: "I am the servant of the Lord, let it be done to me as you have said." She is God's servant as Gabriel and the angels are servants. She obeys as the angels obey. She accepts, acknowledges the power of God and welcomes it within her body, her life, her presence. She seeks only to serve God's mysterious plan for the people, for all of creation. She is the new face of God, and Gabriel bends before that face, honoring the image of God that will give flesh and blood and bone and sinew to God incarnate in humankind.

This is the end of the angels' testing; they have been asked to bow to God incarnated in humanity. This is the obedience the angels learn from a wisp of a girl, a woman bent on obedience, who will gladly disappear into the shadow of the Holy One. Her yes is born of struggle as sure and enduring as Jacob's with the angel, and it will be wrested from her every day of her life. Her agony will be deep and penetrating at the sight of the horrors to come, and she will stand with only the power of God to sustain her. She and her child are filled with the power of the Spirit from the moment she gives over her heart and her life.

When God approached the angels of heaven and asked for their obedience, this was the divine plan. This annunciation is incarnation, liberation and joy; it is the truth of the Holy One, which will exalt and sing and dance closer to heaven because of Mary's belief and submission. The dance rises, continuing the joy and laughter of Sarah, of Hannah, of all the men and women who have waited and staked their lives on freedom. As God bends to the small of the earth to lift truth up, God has taken note of her. With Mary's yes she announces that all the orders of the world will be turned upside down to accommodate the humble, the meek, the lowly, the poor, those hungry for food and justice and the honor of God. All else will be overturned. The revolution of those who are obedient sets in motion the true history of creation and the world. God's Word is sure. God's Word is true.

There is an old story about angels that I first heard from Anthony de Mello. It goes like this:

- Once upon a time, there was a man who was so holy that even the angels rejoiced at the sight of him and wondered what he would do to surprise God next. Even though he was so holy, so like God, he had no idea that he was. He was unself-conscious and aware only of others' needs and the presence of God everywhere. He was so full of gratitude that it overflowed onto everything and into every corner around him.

  After many years the angels decided that they'd like to give him a gift—with God's blessing—in honor of his holiness and in gratitude for the way he reflected the Holy One. They marveled that he looked so deep into the hearts of each person he encountered that he could see God there just as God sees and reaches for the goodness of creation.

  So an angel was dispatched to him. The angel appeared before him, bending low and said: "I have been sent to you by God. Ask for anything and it will be given to you."

  The man hesitated, wondering what in the world he could ask for.

  The angel spoke again: "Do you want the gift of healing?"

  "No," replied the man, "I'd rather that God did the healing and got the credit for it."

  "Would you like to be so holy that others would imitate you and thus bless God and come closer to God?"

  "No," he said again, "that would be terrible for that would make me the center of attention rather than God."

  "Would you like to be a great preacher and reconciler, bringing sinners and lost souls back to the fold?"

  "No, I've always believed that was the work of the Shepherd and that you, the angels, rejoiced exceedingly over each one that came home."

"What do you want then? Please ask for something. We want to give you a gift to honor God in you."

The man thought for a moment, and his face lit up. "I know," he said, "I want the grace of God. For if I have God's favor then I have God's truth and all else besides. I need nothing else."

"But," said the angel, "don't you want some miracle, some blessing as Jacob claimed in his struggle?"

The man thought again: "All right, if I must have some blessing, then give me this: that all the good I do, I will do unawares and no one will know that it was my doing. And so they will bless God for God's divine goodness."

The angel agreed upon such a blessing. It was decreed that the man's shadow would be filled with blessing, and all that he did and said would leave a blessing, but it would always be behind him. He would never know, others would never suspect and God would receive all the glory. And so it has been.

Those who are truly good, those who most resemble God, go about as the shadow of God, filling the earth with holiness and hope and bringing the truth closer to home.

Angels, some say, are shadows of the Most High, shadows of God. Holiness is perhaps shadow play, dancing with God so the earth can be free and the truth can be told. The Word of truth was born to a woman who said simply, "I am the servant of the Lord, let it be done to me as you have said." Then the angel left her, for the truth had been told.

3

RAPHAEL

Companion Angel

Whenever the celestial spirits descend to earth, they clothe themselves in physical things and appear to people in human shape.

—Zohar I, 101a

There is an enchanting though strange story in the Jewish Midrash told in Germany about two sisters, the daughters of a great king, and two angels who come to earth because they are distressed at the amount of evil on the earth. The story takes place in the time before Noah. It addresses the question of why the good and the just seem to have it so hard in the world and yet continue to make choices for the good of others in obedience to the word of God, even at great personal loss. It has intimations of what happens in the Book of Tobit and the situation of the suffering of the just and the visit of an angel who comforts and heals. But there is a great difference: the love of one of the women, one of the sisters, rivals Raphael; it teaches heaven about the meaning of love on earth. It reminds believers of the love of God, who will come to earth as Jesus.

- It was before the great flood of Noah. The earth had grown hard and evil. Two angels especially were horrified at the state of the world. Shemhazai and Azael came before the Holy One and pleaded with Yahweh God to end such wickedness on the earth. How can you tolerate such actions? Those who do good should be rewarded and those who do evil should be punished, or else wickedness will grow and extend its hold over all the earth. Then you will destroy what you have made so that creation can begin anew.

The Holy One pointed out that if angels were on earth, they too would go the way of the world, learning the ways of evil and being caught in its trap. But Yahweh God allowed them to go, disguised as two young men. The two angels hoped to persuade the people of earth to turn from their evil ways and learn to live with justice, in peace. Before they left heaven they made two promises to God: first, that they would not reveal the secrets of heaven to anyone; and second, that they would not marry.

They arrived in a kingdom that had two beautiful sisters, Ishtar and Naamah, daughters of the king. The two angels promptly fell in love with the two sisters, Shemhazai with Ishtar and Azael with Naamah. The two angels offered to amuse the king with feats of mirage and magic. Shemhazai went first. He stood still and then turned himself into an eagle. He flew off and returned with a rose in his beak. He landed on Ishtar's arm and dropped the flower in her lap, then turned back into a man. Next came Azael's turn. He conjured up the sea with roaring waves. The walls of the palace disappeared and water flooded in. In the midst of the terror, he turned and smiled at Naamah, and instantly the water disappeared. It was just a mirage. Both young men stood before the two sisters and bowed. When they swept off their great hats with flourishes, out fell cascades of sweet-smelling gardenias that covered the feet of the young women. Both angels were helplessly in love.

The king realized that with these two young men married to his daughters he could rule any kingdom, so he promptly offered his daughters in marriage. The two angels, smitten with the sisters' beauty, forgot their promise to God not to marry on earth. The wedding date was set.

That night Ishtar was visited by Enoch, a messenger of God, in a dream. She listened and learned that the two young men were really angels sent to earth by God and that they both intended to break their vows by marrying the two sisters. If they did, their children would be a race that would do great evil on the earth, a race of giants, cruel and inhuman. They would fill the world with sin and evil, and God would destroy the earth.

Ishtar knew what she had to do. With tears in her eyes, she told Enoch the messenger that she would not marry her beloved Shemhazai. Thus she would do her part to save the earth from such a fate. She could not bear that her love would cause the destruction of the world.

When Ishtar awoke, she told her sister, Naamah, of the dream. They must, she said, refuse to marry Shemhazai and Azael. Her sister Naamah, however, refused to believe her sister's dream. She was not about to give up her beloved to save the earth in response to some crazy dream. No matter how much Ishtar pleaded, Naamah would not believe her.

Exhausted, Ishtar fell back to sleep and dreamed again of Enoch. He came to her, telling her he knew of her sister's refusal. He sought to console Ishtar, saying if only one sister married an angel the horror that would come upon the world would be lessened. God would flood the earth and destroy it, but some creatures would be saved. Because of her sacrifice and love, one pair of every kind of animal, fish and bird would be spared. From this remnant the world would be renewed.

Ishtar awoke again in the cold light of dawn and went to Shemhazai and told him she knew who he was and that she could not marry him, though she loved him with all her heart and soul. Shemhazai was repentant and in horror realized that he had been about to break his word to the Holy One. The two of them embraced for the last time and parted as beloveds still.

Heaven watched and the angels rejoiced at Ishtar's love and sacrifice. Here was a woman who cared more for the earth and its people than for her own personal happiness. The angels asked a favor of God: to remember her and to share her love and sacrifice in a way that others would know that she held back the hand of God's justice and let mercy stream into the world even in the midst of a flood of destruction. And so God made her the morning star, which remains after the cold dawn of the moon disappears to keep the rising sun company.

Naamah married Azael, and their children were the dreaded and wicked Nephillim. They brought such evil to the world that the Holy One was obliged to flood the earth. But God spared Noah and all the creatures in the ark because of Ishtar's compassion for the human race. And the morning star stays in the sky as a reminder of the power of love and the depth of sacrifice needed in the struggle between good and evil. It is a reminder that we too are called to be just, even to put aside our own happiness if necessary. Those who get up early enough to see the morning star may learn to see the angels of the world and recognize those that are fallen and those sent by God. But more important, they can learn to remember that it is because of good and just men and women like Ishtar that we are here at all to gaze at the heavens and bless God for creation and life. It is said that angels come and go, visiting, but humankind stays on earth.

Tobit and his son Tobias, in the Book of Tobit, are ordinary folk privileged to receive a visit from the angel Raphael, one of the seven who stand before the face of God. Raphael embodies God's graciousness and healing, which is the meaning of his name.

The Book of Tobit is the story of a Jew attempting to live in exile from his beloved Israel. He is part of the Diaspora tradition of the Jewish community, which seeks to return to the heart of its religion and life in Jerusalem and remains faithful in spite of being in foreign lands and often persecuted for the practice of its religion. This particular man is Tobit (Tobias) of the tribe of Naphtali, who was deported from Galilee in the reign of Shalmaneser, king of Assyria.

Tobit describes himself: "I, Tobit, have walked in the ways of truth and justice all the days of my life; I have given many alms to my brethren and to those of my countrymen who were deported with me to Nineveh, a city in the country of the Assyrians." He has honored truth and justice whether the way lay in bounty or in hardship, at home in Israel or sojourning in a strange land. He goes to Jerusalem to sacrifice and tithe, and even now as a prisoner he is gracious to the widow, orphan and poor who are in more dire straits than he is himself. In time he rises to power as the treasurer in the court of Shalmaneser. Then Shalmaneser dies and his son, Sennacherib, becomes king. And the lives of the Jews in exile become more and more difficult.

Nonetheless, Tobit continues to practice almsgiving, giving his bread to the hungry, his garments to those who were naked and if he saw anyone of his tribe dead and his body thrown over the ramparts of Nineveh he would bury him secretly. Eventually someone betrays him to the king and he is forced into hiding. Tobit loses everything, including his wife Anna and his only son, Tobias. But the intrigue of the city changes with the killing of Sennacherib by his sons and Tobit returns, once again to rise to power.

Tobit's family gathers for the feast of Pentecost. In the midst of the feast word comes that one of his relatives has been killed and his body thrown outside into the public square. Immediately Tobit leaves the meal and brings the body back to bury. He eats his food in sorrow and mourning and remembers the words of Amos, "All your songs will be turned into lamentations" and he weeps (Tob. 2:6). After sunset he buries the man and then sleeps outside because of the heat. While he sleeps, the sparrows' droppings fall into his eyes and he is blinded.

For four years Tobit suffers blindness. He is helpless and endures the ridicule of his neighbors and kinsmen. They speak ill of him for his good deed of burying the dead: "He no longer fears to be put to death for doing that; he had to flee but look he is again burying the dead." His wife Anna works as a weaver, but they struggle in their poverty, slavery and oppression, and in the shame their own people cast upon them. The unjust reproaches cause him great distress, and he casts his care on God. Tobit cries out to God for death, for freedom, remembering that this time of trial is just because of all the sins of the people and their unfaithfulness to God.

Suddenly the story jumps to Ecbatana in Media, to the daughter of Ragouel, Sara, who is sore distressed and thinking to hang herself. She has attempted marriage seven times and each time on her wedding night the demon Asmodeus has killed her husband before the marriage is consummated. She is humiliated, shunned and mocked, insulted, and yet, even in her pain, she thinks of her father and cannot commit suicide. She turns to the window and cries out to God for death or for freedom from her misery. This is the setting for the appearance of the archangel Raphael:

> The Lord in his glory heard the prayer of Tobit and of Sara and he sent Raphael to heal them both—to give back his sight to Tobit and to give Sara, the daughter of Ragouel, to Tobit's son Tobias, as his wife. Also, Raphael would enchain the wicked demon Asmodeus so that Sara would be the wife of Tobias. (Tob. 3:16–17)

It seems that distance is of no account; all are interwoven in the presence of God, who sees affliction and hears the prayers of those in need and distress, especially those who are just and good and yet oppressed by both outsiders and their own kin. Tobit calls his son Tobias to him and tells him of money deposited with friends in Media, but first he tells him how to live—a wayfarer's code of honor (Tob. 4:5–19). In addition, he offers the practical advice that he should marry one who belongs to their tribe and those of their ancestors and prophets so that they and their children might be blessed on the land and in the covenant. In this way, both God and those who have gone before in faith are honored. Tobias is told to find a companion to travel with him to Gabael at Rages in Media to get the money.

And Tobias goes out and promptly finds the angel Raphael.

Tobias went to look for a man and he found Raphael. Raphael was an angel but Tobias did not know it. Tobias said to Raphael, "Can you go with me to Rages in Media? Do you know the place?" The angel said to Tobias, "I will go with you. I know the way and I have even spent a night with your kinsman, Gabael." (Tob. 5:4–6)

Raphael, brought in to meet Tobit, describes himself as "Azarias, the son of Ananias the Great, one of your kinsmen." He is brother, part of the family; in fact, Ananias used to travel with Tobit to Jerusalem when they went up for sacrifice and tithe. Ananias is faithful to the covenant of the Lord. They settle on wages and after more assurances from Raphael, set out, with Tobias's dog following.

Thus the journey begins that will join these two families. It is Raphael who will tie the knot, but it is God who sets up the marriage and uses the tribulations of each of the families to strengthen the bonds. This is the way of the Lord: the way of the Lord is in the world and through the world but not of the world. It follows another "map," and those who are just and righteous, careful of the poor, giving alms even in their own hard times will find friends and companions on the way, perhaps even angels.

The journey is from one place to another, but the traveling is just as important as the destination. The journey is preparation for what follows. The first evening they stop at the River Tigris to spend the night. As Tobias is washing his feet, a great fish rises out of the water and tries to swallow his foot.

> Raphael said to Tobias, "Catch that fish!" Tobias seized the fish and drew it to land. Raphael then said to Tobias, "Open the fish, take out its heart, liver and gall and put them away carefully. Throw away the intestines. The gall, the heart and the liver of this fish are useful remedies." Tobias did as the angel told him. He opened up the fish, kept the gall, the heart and the liver; then they cooked the fish and ate it.
>
> Then the two of them continued their journey until they reached Media. Tobias said to Raphael, "Friend Azarias, what remedy is there in the heart, the liver and the gall of the fish?" Raphael said to him, "If you burn the heart and the liver in the presence of a man or woman who is tormented by a devil or an evil spirit, their torments will cease. As for the gall, if you smear it on a man whose eyes are covered with a white film, his eyes will be cured."
>
> When they had entered Media and were already approaching Ecbatana, Raphael said to Tobias, "Friend, we shall spend the night at the house of Ragouel. He is a relative of yours. He has no son, just an only daughter called Sara. I will speak to him and ask that he give her to you as your wife. You are the one who is nearest of kin and free to marry her. You alone are of her tribe and you should inherit her father's goods. The girl is wise, good, courageous and very beautiful and her father is a good man. So listen, friend, tonight we will marry you to her. When we return from Rages, we shall take her with us and introduce her into your home. She belongs to you rather than to any other man according to the Law of

Moses, and any trespasser would die. So I know that Ragouel will not give her to any other man." (Tob. 6:4–13)

Raphael dispenses the folk wisdom of medicine and acts as marriage broker, reminding Tobias of the Law of Moses, even giving an explanation for the deaths of Sara's previous seven husbands—none of them was the one that God intended for her. It is an ancient tradition in the Jewish community that it is the task of God to arrange the marriages of the people. God contemplates this work on the Sabbath, looking to see who belongs to whom and how the divine plan will be worked out in the world with grace and truth; it is a work that God delights in. The ancient tradition says that God presides at all marriages. In fact, the Midrash tells stories of Yahweh God braiding Eve's hair on her wedding day and preparing her for Adam. Marriages are lasting, true ways of honoring the Lord, as is the Sabbath itself.

Tobias is not quick to take to the idea of marrying Sara. He doesn't relish sharing the same fate as her seven previous husbands. He reminds Raphael that he is his father's only son; he fears death, but also fears causing his father and mother to die of grief on his account. But Raphael knows the way through this quagmire too:

The angel said to Tobias, "Do you not remember your father's advice to marry a woman of your own tribe? Well, listen to me, my friend. She will be your wife. Do not worry about the demon as this very night she will be your wife.

"When you enter the wedding chamber you will take some glowing embers of incense and you will put on top of them part of the heart and liver of the fish. As soon as the fire begins to smoke, the demon will smell it and flee, never to return. And when you go to Sara, stand up together and call on the all-merciful God. He will keep you safe because he has compassion. Do not be afraid, because from all eternity Sara has been destined to be your wife. You will save her, and she will go with us. And I am sure that she will bear you children."

When Tobias heard Raphael's words, he loved Sara and his heart became strongly attached to her. (Tob. 6:16–19)

Just listening to the word of the Lord in the angel's mouth, listening to his friend and companion on the way, expands Tobias's heart. His trust in Raphael is strong. Raphael is his teacher, mentor, confidante and counselor.

They arrived at Ragouel's house and are welcomed by his family and introduced to his wife Edna and their daughter Sara and fed with great kindness. Relaxing before the meal, after the rites of hospitality are finished, Tobias tells Raphael to bring up the matter that they decided upon on the road. Ragouel is delighted to give Sara in marriage to Tobias but leery that Tobias will make it through the night. Still, he marries them:

"Take her from now on; I give her to you according to the Law of Moses and you have to understand that God himself gives her to you. Receive your kinswoman, from now on you are her brother and she is your sister. She is yours from today and forever. Now God will bless you this night and may he give you both his mercy and peace." (Tob. 7:11b)

While they eat, Sara's mother Edna prepares the bed chamber and Sara begins to cry. But Edna dries her daughter's tears and encourages her. After the meal, Tobias is escorted to Sara's room and does as Raphael told him. Then he and Sara pray together and retire for the night.

Much to everyone's surprise Tobias makes it through the night unharmed, and in the morning there is great rejoicing. A proper wedding of fourteen days of feasting and celebration ensues. Ragouel gives Tobias and Sara half of his possessions; the other half will come to them when he and Edna die. They are now one family. And Ragouel declares: "You will bring joy to my daughter, who

has suffered so much" (Tob. 8:20). While the wedding is being celebrated, Raphael goes on to Gabael and recovers the money they
had been sent to retrieve.

Meanwhile Tobit and Anna wait for Tobias to return, counting
the days. Anna begins to weep and mourn his death, refusing to eat
or sleep. Tobit tries to comfort her, but she pushes him away, crying incessantly. Tobias too counts the days, knowing his parents
will be worried, and they set off as soon as the fourteen days are
accomplished. Sara leaves her parents' home and returns with
Tobias and Raphael to Nineveh. Once again it is Raphael who
speaks confidently to Tobias and suggests that he and Tobias go on
ahead to prepare the house and to care for Tobit. He reminds
Tobias to bring with him the gall of the fish. Again, Tobias's dog
accompanies them.

It is Anna who sees them coming, and she rushes out to meet
them. While Tobias and Raphael are still walking along the road,
Raphael speaks to Tobias reassuringly: "I am sure that your father
will regain his sight. Rub his eyes with the fish gall and when he
feels his eyes itching, he will rub them and the film will come away
like scales from his eyes. He will regain his sight and see the light"
(Tob. 11:7–8).

Tobias obeys Raphael, and Tobit can once again see his son. He
rejoices and blesses God. Then Tobias shares with them the good
news that he is married and his wife is on the outskirts of the city,
waiting to be welcomed into their home. It is a day of great rejoicing, not just for Anna and Tobit but for all their relatives in the city.
The second wedding celebration lasts another week. After the feasting, Tobit calls Tobias and reminds him to pay his traveling companion his wages and to throw in something extra for all his service
and compassion and wisdom. Tobias says, "What shall I give him?
It would not be too much if I were to give him half of what I have
brought back since he has brought me home again safe and sound.
He has taken care of my wife and he helped me to get back the

money. He has also cured your blindness." The old man said, "That amount would be well justified in his case" (Tob. 12:1–4). So the angel is called to receive half of what Tobias has brought back with him. And then Raphael takes Tobit and Tobias aside to speak to them alone. First he teaches them wisdom and reflects on their lives. Then, hiding nothing from them, he tells them his true name and who he really is—so much more than a companion on the way.

> "I will hide nothing from you. Yes, I have said that it is good to keep the secrets of kings but to make known publicly the glorious works of God. Tobit, when you and your daughter-in-law Sara prayed, I kept the remembrance of your prayer before the Holy One; when you, Tobit, buried the dead, I was with you in the same way; and when you did not hesitate to rise up and leave your meal in order to hide the dead man, your good deed did not go unnoticed because I was with you.
>
> "Well, God sent me to cure you and also to cure Sara, your daughter-in-law. I am Raphael, one of the seven holy angels who present the prayers of holy people and who stand before the glory of God." (Tob. 12:11–15)

Tobit and Tobias respond with fear and trembling—the usual response of the righteous to the known presence of an angel—and they fall on the ground on their faces, seized with terror. But Raphael once again calms and eases their minds. Then he disappears.

The journey of Raphael to the earth is done; the work completed. The journey of Tobias to Ragouel's house both to meet and marry Sara and to collect the money owed his father in Media is finished, and so his companion returns home to the heavens to stand before the face of God. He has obeyed God completely. He has cured Tobit of his blindness and released Sara from her bondage to the demon Asmodeus. He has lifted the shame of both families and made them one, strengthening the covenant of the Lord. By vindicating the righteousness of the poor and the just, he has given honor to God. As always he has lifted the prayers of the holy people of God, keeping the remembrance of their good deeds and their prayers before God. What he has always done in heaven he has been sent to complete here on earth. Then he returns to bless God. In response to knowing the presence of the angel and the salvation sent to them, Tobit composes a prayer in ecstasy and joy, blessing God, who lives and reigns for all ages.

Tobit then exhorts Jerusalem and its inhabitants to rejoice and praise God so that the Temple might be restored and so that God can gladden the exiles upon their return. He prophesies that many nations will go to Jerusalem bearing gifts and that once again the just will be gathered home. In the tradition of the great prophets he describes the rebuilding of Jerusalem in glowing terms, crying out that even her streets will cry "Alleluia" and all will praise God saying: "Blessed be God who has glorified you forever."

The interactions with Raphael have taught him how to pray. He calls his entire nation back to the Holy One, reminding the people of the great works of God and their own need for remembrance and repentance so that God may show them all mercy. The experience of having met Raphael has enlarged his already great heart to reach out further to all the exiles and those in the future who will know the salvation of God and the reestablishment of the Temple and the ingathering of the people of God. It is a song of pure thanksgiving.

Tobit grows old and his wisdom is that of a sage and prophet. When he is very old he calls Tobias to him and sends him to Media, for it will be safer there. He is mindful of the prophet Nahum's words, foretelling the destruction of Nineveh and Assyria. He knows that there will be peace for a short time and then all the people in the land of Israel will be dispersed. Israel will be emptied. Jerusalem and Samaria will be desolate. The Temple will be burned and left in ruins. Eventually the people will return from captivity and rebuild the Temple, but not as magnificently as the first. Yet one day all nations will stream to the city of Jerusalem and the new Temple, and they will praise the God of justice. It will come to pass.

When Tobit and Anna die, their son Tobias buries them and moves to Media. He and Sara settle in Ecbatana near Ragouel, where Tobias takes care of his parents-in-law as faithfully and carefully as he tended his own parents. He lives until he is one hundred and twenty-seven years old and so sees the downfall of Nineveh when Nebuchadnezzar destroys the city. The Ninevites and the Assyrians are reduced to slavery and the currents of the world shift according to the foretelling of the prophets—the hidden wisdom of the Lord God. And Tobias "blessed the Lord God forever" (Tob. 14:15).

The Book of Tobit could easily be called the Book of Raphael, except the focus is never on the angels. Once again the angels reiterate that they serve the Holy One, obeying the Lord's commands about earth. Although they dwell before the face of God, in the presence of God, they visit earth to do the bidding of God and serve God's holy people. Earth is never their dwelling place. They slip in and out of earth's history on the word of God. They are servants of God, bending to earth to help the children of God.

The experience of encountering an angel is for the benefit of the earth as it seeks to fulfill the command of creation and return to its original blessing and wholeness. The visitation of an angel changes history, reroutes its course and sets those who are faithful to the Law of God and the care of the poor and the doing of justice on the way that leads to safety, security, peace and the presence of God—even in the midst of oppression, slavery, injustice and personal suffering at the hands of others, even demons. All creation serves God and those who belong to God in obedience to the divine law and covenant.

Raphael is truly an angel, existing to praise and bless the Holy One. Raphael's Hebrew name means "Heal me, O God!" Everything connected to Raphael's presence on earth is bound to healing. There is the obvious physical healing of Tobit's blindness. There is the healing of Sara's shame and terror at the death of her seven husbands and her torment by a demon. There is the overcoming of desolation—the healing that marriage brings to those who are separate and alone, and the healing of separation between families and the dispersed and scattered nation of Israel in the bondage of slavery. All of this healing is in response to works of justice and mercy, such as almsgiving to the poor and less fortunate and the burying of the dead, especially those killed by enemies of God.

Raphael hears and holds the lamentations and desperate cries of those who seek to obey the law of God in the midst of the unfaithfulness of neighbors and kinsmen and in the midst of foreigners who belittle their faith and its practice in a foreign land. It is Raphael's work to hold the prayers of the holy ones of God and keep them before the face of God until the time God wishes to answer them in the larger vision of creation and history.

Raphael is a visitor, a fleeting though ever-faithful friend, a companion on the way, choosing only to reveal his true identity when his work is finished. His most cherished and often forgotten gift to Tobit, Tobias and Sara is the gift of how to pray, how to stand before God and bless God always, in spite of hardships, trial and being shamed by others. He brings the gifts of consistency, of enduring grace and thanksgiving, acknowledging God as the Holy One, the sustainer of all things and all people. Raphael's gift, in short, is the gift of love: friendship and companionship, marriage and service in healing and encouragement. He gives heart to those in distress and need. In his time with Raphael, Tobias learns of friendship and companionship, and so he knows how to love Sara as companion and friend, sister and wife. Together they know the love that prays and opposes evil. They obey the wisdom of their ancestors, continuing the practices of justice and almsgiving in the care of the widow, the orphan and the victims caught in the unjust decrees and practices of those who do not believe in the God of Israel. They know the love of family, of children and generations that share together the unfolding of God's history, which is always true to God's word. They know the love of God that is expressed by an angel, one created to stand together with those who bless God and hold up the prayers of those caught in earth's tangle of hate and might.

Raphael is the patron of travelers, gypsies, healers, fishers, the blind, marriage counselors, lovers and women who need to be protected from evil and shame. He teaches friends and lovers how to stand together, pray and make it through the night of terror without being harmed, to become true companions on the way together. He teaches those who are open to him, as Tobias and Sara were, to pray, to relate together with God as their first companion and to set priorities in their marriages and families and public lives. He is friend to the old and the young, parents and children, in-laws and far-flung families, men and women.

Often Raphael is depicted as a vagabond, with fishing pole over his shoulder and a dog at his heels as he travels the road. His is the wisdom of the road; he is the wayfarer who uses his knowledge to help and to heal and to assuage the loneliness of others. He is friend to those who are the friends of God, sent for a while to ease their loneliness and sense of distance from God. He overcomes their desire for death, which they experience because of the lack of support and dignity that they encounter as they attempt to be just in the face of adversity. His medicines are ordinary: fish innards, prayer, love, thanksgiving to God.

No demon, unjust situation, violent government or personal problem can stand against the power of Raphael's wisdom. He gives hope, a future, release from the grip of death and suffering. Raphael is "the alms of God," the Holy One's presence drawing nearer to us for a while. This presence heals and converts, transforms and illuminates everyone that it touches. Raphael is the blessing God sends to those who, like the Holy One, care for the poorest and those most despairing in this vale of tears.

The Book of Tobit, and the appearance of Raphael, is a primer on how to live in a culture that is not conducive to the worship of the true God or the faithful practice of one's religion. It is full of practical suggestions on how not to be assimilated into the prevailing culture and how to resist governments and policies that evoke hostility to piety. Since Tobit cannot get to Jerusalem and worship as he should, he worships God where he can—in the poor and with the ritual of almsgiving. He is careful to make sure that his only son Tobias marries someone who is of like mind and intent on the priorities of the covenant and not of the culture. This faithfulness to God eventually will restore the right practice of religion and the Temple itself.

Tobit even practices civil disobedience by burying the bodies of those the king kills, infuriating the king, much as many people of Central and South America bury the bodies of those dumped along the roadside who have been murdered by military forces. The reality and presence of death calls for justice and compassion, but practicing these does not preclude personal, ignominious suffering—going blind from bird droppings!

Even the names of the characters in this story are revelatory: *Tobit* and *Tobias* are derivatives from the Hebrew for "the Lord is my good." *Raguol* means "friend of God"; another variation, Raguel, is the name of the archangel in 1 Enoch 20:4, 23:4.[1] *Raphael* is "God heals," and *Azariah*, the name he assumes as Tobias's companion, is derived from "God has helped" or "God is gracious."

The women's names are also symbolically connected to the past history of Israel. *Anna* is kin to Hannah, who prays to God for a child and faces many difficulties having a child, even the scorn of the priests (1 Sam. 1–2). Sara is namesake of Abraham's wife, barren of children except for the promise of God, delivered by angels. *Edna* is from a Hebrew word used in the book of Genesis to describe Sarah's comment when she hears the news that she will conceive a son in her old age: "Sarah laughed to herself saying: 'Now that I am old and worn and my husband is an old man, am I to have this pleasure?" (Gen. 18:12). *Edna* is that term for "pleasure."

Everything in the story—names, details, geography, distances—reveals and conceals, for it is a story of exile, of being lost and away from home, away from Israel, the Temple and the right ordering of relationships, families and society. Raphael is the companion of the lost, the wandering, the homeless, those bereft of comfort and a dwelling place secure in this world, those without land, home or future except in the mystery of God's care for the lost and wayfaring. Raphael is companion to those alone and lonely, without dignity or hope of marriage, children and security in old age, without friends in this world because they seek to be faithful to God and justly care for those less fortunate than themselves. He travels the road with those who seek to be human in a world that dehumanizes and robs men and women of their dignity through politics, displacement of peoples and tyranny.

Tobit is a book of hope, a way to walk in the paths of justice and peace, blessing and enduring grace, knowing that the angels hold our prayers in remembrance before God and accompany us, often unknowingly, in obeying the will of God. We never know who is by our side. No matter what we are suffering publicly and privately, we are in the presence of God and God sends an angel to heal, with graciousness.

But we must remember to act like God: give alms. In the words of the prophet Micah, "You have been told, O man, what is good and what Yahweh requires of you: to do justice, to love mercy, and to walk humbly with your God" (Mic. 6:8).

There are always angels in disguise who travel with us, befriending us, healing us, going fishing with us, dispensing wisdom, arranging marriages, opening the eyes of the blind, protecting us from the evils of hedonism and demons—all that seeks to hinder us from living holy lives.

NOTE

1. 1 Enoch is part of the *Pseudepigrapha,* a collection of books that include many of the Hebrew and Christian scriptures, such as Isaiah and Ezra, as well as other books such as Solomon, Abraham, Moses, Baruch, 1 and 2 Enoch, the Martyrdom and Ascension of Isaiah and the Life of Adam and Eve. Pieces of these books, especially 1 Enoch, were found among the Dead Sea Scrolls.

4

URIEL

Archangel of Death and Conversion

It was the first day in time, the first full day in exile from the Garden of Eden. Adam and Eve had wandered, though not far from the flaming sword, always keeping it in sight. And then the sun began to sink lower and lower in the sky and dusk came. The sunset was magnificent, a sky full of burning fires and embers, but then the darkness crept in. Adam and Eve were terrified, huddled together in fear as the earth cooled down and it grew cold. What was happening? Was Yahweh God still angry and punishing them further? Had the light disappeared forever never to be seen again? Were they cursed to live in the dark in their exile?

But Yahweh God looked on his creatures with pity and gave them two flints to rub together. One flint was darkness and the other was death; when rubbed together they produced fire. The fire kept them through the long first night and the ones that followed, easing their fears and giving them hope. They could sit by the fire and remember the stronger light. The sages say that this is the meaning of the psalm:

Shall I say, "Let darkness hide me, and light become night about me?"

But darkness for you is not dark and night for you shines as the day....

You have scrutinized my actions and all my days are ordained by you; you have recorded them all in your book before any one of them ever existed. (Ps. 139:11–12, 16)

Adam and Eve were reassured that the darkness would be overcome by the sun's rising and that dawn would follow after the coldest, darkest part of the night. And so, for the Jewish community the day begins at sundown. The remembrance of the Sabbath rest, the feast of Passover and all other celebrations begin at night when the third star rises in the heavens. All Jews dedicate themselves to kindling the light in all things on earth and so to drive out the darkness of sin and evil, to kindle a fire upon the earth that will summon the presence of the Messiah, the Sun of Justice.

But there were two flints; besides darkness there was death. Often the Angel of Death has been associated with Satan, the Prince of Darkness, but in both the Jewish and Christian traditions there is a radical separation between the two spirits. Satan is evil personified, an adversarial force that both predates the creation of human beings and is experienced in the freedom given to humans. We are responsible for the evil that we choose, tolerate and live with in collusion. However, death, like the coming of night that follows day, has become part of the pattern of life, of what it means to be human after the fall. Death is the fulfillment, the completion of life, which consists of being born and dying and all that bridges those two events. But there is death that is natural and death that is chosen, planned, executed, violent, unnecessary and not natural —and that death is evil, is sin. The death we will look at in this chapter is the work of the Angel of Death, Uriel. It is the death that draws us out of life and into the Light.

The Angel of Death, Uriel (or Phanuel) is called by name— along with Michael, Gabriel and Raphael—in 1 Enoch.

I saw them standing—on the four wings of the Lord of the Spirits—and saw four other faces among those who do not slumber, and I came to know their names, which the angel who came with me revealed to me…. "The first one is the merciful and forbearing Michael; the second one, who is set over all disease and every wound of the children of the people, is Raphael; and the third, who is set over all exercise of strength is Gabriel; and the fourth, who is set over all actions of repentance unto the hope of those who would inherit the eternal life, is Phanuel (Uriel) by name." (1 Enoch 40:2–10)

These four angels are the closest to God, forming an inner square around God's throne. 1 Enoch also adds three more angels: Sariel, whose work is unknown; Jeremiel, who is in charge of the souls of the underworld; and Raguel, who takes vengeance on evildoers on behalf of those who struggle for light and justice. (These other three angels are a bit different in the Eastern spirituality of the church.)

We fear the coming of Uriel, the Angel of Death. No one wants to die. We cling to life as our dearest possession. Many stories are told of attempts to escape death. And along with the tales are bound ancient traditions that the Angel of Death can't take someone while he is touching the Torah or studying the scrolls of the words of life. It is told in the Midrash that even Moses sought to escape death.

- When Yahweh came to Moses and took him up a mountain to show him the Promised Land and to tell him that he would not go into it, Moses said nothing. But he waited for his opportunity.

    When the time came for him to die, he drew a magic circle around himself and threw his prayers into heaven. God immediately ordered the gates of heaven shut tight against Moses' prayers. They battered the walls and gates with such noise and ferocity that even the angels were shaken and frightened. But it was to no avail. God held firm. Moses must die like all humans.

Moses debated God and told him that in refusing to let him into the Promised Land, God was betraying his own word given to the people. But God responded to this accusation by saying that Moses would be rewarded in the world to come. So Moses tried another tack. He started writing out a Torah scroll, and the Angel of Death, sent by God to take Moses' soul, was afraid to approach him. When God told the angel to go again and lay claim to Moses' soul, Moses beat the Angel of Death severely with his staff!

And so, finally, God himself took Moses' soul with sweet words and the kiss of death. Moses escaped the Angel of Death but not death itself.

The angels dug the grave and laid the body to rest, hidden in secret in the mountains overlooking the Jordan River and the route the Israelites took into the Promised Land. And Yahweh God cried and mourned the death of Moses.

This Yahweh God, who brought forth the children of Israel out of bondage in Egypt and through the waters of the Red Sea, is midwife and mourner. God cares about us from the beginning—in drawing us forth out of the waters of the womb to laying us in the ground, the womb that receives us back until forever.

The Midrash tells that David also sought to live forever, or at least to keep extending his time on earth.

- King David, in conversation with the Lord, blessed be his name, asked how long he would live, but Yahweh God refused to tell him. It is not given for humans to know the span of their years. But David pressed, saying: "Well, at least tell me on which day I am to die." That the Lord revealed to him: "It will be on a Sabbath." And David, already planning on living long and outwitting the Angel of Death, asked, "Please, let me die on a Sunday, so that I do not take away from the joy of the day of blessing and rest." But the mind of Yahweh was not to be changed. Yahweh explained to David: "It cannot be. The reign of your son Solomon must begin on Sunday and the kingdom of one must not overlap that of the other even for one second. It is decreed."

So, following an ancient tradition, every Sabbath, King David studied Torah the whole day long so that the Angel of Death couldn't touch him.

The Sabbath came on which he was to die. The Angel of Death came, but David was studying, deep in his texts and books. Uriel couldn't touch his soul. The angel watched David from a distance and thought how to take his soul, for so he was commanded by God. Then he smiled, for he had hit upon a plan.

David had a garden full of plants and flowers from all over the world, and he loved that garden. So the angel went and began shaking the trees. David looked up from his studies, concerned, and ran out into his garden. He was curious to know who was shaking the trees from above, and so he climbed a ladder. But the ladder broke under him, and so the Angel of Death thus took his soul. And David was given his place in Paradise.[1]

The Angel of Death serves God as any other angel does, obeying the will of the Holy One. The Angel of Death is needed in the world, part of the pattern of life and death, blossoming and decay, rise and fall. Death is an intimate and necessary part of all life, all creatures. In 1 Enoch, the four angels seize those condemned on the day of judgment and cast them into the furnace so that the Lord of the Spirits may take vengeance on them for their oppressive deeds. Michael the archangel speaks: "For indeed human beings were not created but to be like angels, permanently to maintain pure and righteous lives. Death, which destroys everything, would have not touched them, had it not been through their knowledge by which they shall perish; death is now eating us by means of this power" (1 Enoch 69:11).

The tree of the knowledge of good and evil was also the tree of death. Eating the fruit of the tree brought forth death, both the death that serves life and completes it and the death chosen with forethoughts of evil and malice. Much of scripture seeks to give meaning to the reality of death, which is experienced not as the bridge into everlasting life, but as horror, brutality, cold-blooded hate, destruction, rage, defiance of creation and the rejection of the value of life itself. This death seems to be the work of injustice and evil. The heart of the Book of Job addresses this issue of the suffering of the just and the apparent rise of those who practice evil. The cruelty, inhumanity and destructiveness of human beings seem stronger than the goodness in God's creatures who seek to obey the will of the One who gives life. Is there no justice, no restoration, no restitution? The long dialogue between God and Job is in response to this impassioned cry for meaning. God responds to Job, but does not answer his question.

> Have the gates of death been shown to you?
> Have you seen the gates of Shadow?
> Have you an idea of the breadth of the earth?
> Tell me, if you know all this.
>
> Where is the way to the home of light,
> and where does darkness dwell? (Job 38:17–19)

God will not give Job the knowledge that he cries out for in suffering and misery. That, it seems, is not an answer that is given to humans. It belongs to the secret mystery of God. This refusal to answer the question is repeated in Uriel's message to Ezra:

> "Your understanding has utterly failed regarding this world, and do you think you can comprehend the way of the Most High?...I have been sent to show you three problems. If you can solve one of them for me, I also will show you the way you desire to see, and will teach you why the heart is evil.... Go,

weigh for me the weight of fire, or measure for me a blast of wind, or call back for me the day that is past." (4 Ezra 4:2–5)

Ezra is trying to deal with the horror of the destruction of the second Temple by the Romans in 66–70 CE, the terrible siege, the slaughter of its inhabitants, and forced march in slavery and humiliation back to Rome. Ezra, like Job and all those who have suffered at the hands of invading armies, destructive forces, vindictiveness, hate and raging evil needs a lifeline to hold to in order to continue living and believing. Uriel, speaking to Ezra, provides that lifeline to the people who believe and remain faithful in the midst of persecution, torture, slavery and death:

> For this is the way of which Moses, while he was alive, spoke to the people, saying "Choose for yourself life, that you may live!" But they did not believe him, or the prophets after him…. Therefore there shall not be grief at their damnation, so much as joy over those to whom salvation is assured. (4 Ezra 7:129–31)

It is decreed. Yahweh God is a God of mercy and compassion, but also of justice and judgment. God is Elohim, king on the throne of justice, and Adonai, the compassionate one, on the seat of mercy. There is death that comes at the hand of the Angel of Death, and there is death that comes at the hand of humans who do not serve and obey the will of the Holy One. That second death will be judged severely, for it is insult to God, both disobedience and usurping of the power of the Most High; it is work in the service of Satan, the one who hinders life and creation.

The Jewish tradition is full of stories of those who seek to outwit or put off the Angel of Death because of love or devotion, and these stories teach the underlying bases for how to live. This one is a Moroccan folktale told by Dov Noy:

- A man and wife had been married only a year, and on their anniversary the man went out into the forest to cut wood for the stove. His wife followed him. It was an eerie day, with little or no sun, hidden behind thick ominous clouds. Even the forest seemed unnaturally quiet—no birds, only the sound of their footsteps. At noon, the Angel of Death appeared in the forest, heading for the woman's husband. He came with his sickle, his great slaughterer's sword and waved it over the head of the man, who fell at his feet, dead. The woman cried out in distress and turned on the Angel of Death, fearlessly arguing with him: "I demand that you tell me why you have robbed me of my husband, my life? The psalms say that man's years on the earth are seventy or eighty if he is lucky. My beloved is only twenty-one. Why have you come for him?"

The answer was simple: "Woman, it is the will of the Holy One, the Creator, who gives and takes life. I only obey."

The woman was not to be deterred. "If that is so, then I demand that you grant me my only wish." The Angel of Death answered: "I will do whatever you may ask, except for one thing: I cannot restore your husband's life."

"I will not ask that," she answered. "What I ask is that you restore my father-in-law's sight. He is blind."

"I will do as you wish," spoke the angel.

"I want your word," she said, "that my father-in-law will see his grandson or great-grandson playing at his feet."

"It will be as you ask," said the angel. "Now go from me."

But the woman stood her ground.

"I am the wife of my father-in-law's only child. I am the only one who can give him grandchildren and great-grand-children, a way into the future. If you really mean to honor your word to me then you must restore my husband to life—there is no other way for my father-in-law to see his children's children. It is said that one who saves even one soul, one child of Israel, preserves and saves the whole nation. If you rob me of my husband, you rob me of my children and my father-in-law of his grandchildren and the promise of the Holy One to his people in the covenant. If you do not restore my husband to me, then you will have broken your word and you will have robbed me and my family of a place in the world to come."

The Angel of Death was stunned. Her logic was impeccable. What could he do? How could he explain it to the Holy One? But, he agreed. And the man stood upon his feet, before his wife once again. They returned to their house, clinging to each other in relief and joy and found their father-in-law praying, reciting the blessing: "Blessed be He who opens the eyes of the blind." They added their own blessings in a long litany and told the story down through the lives of their children and grandchildren and great-great grandchildren, blessing the God of Life unto even this generation. And they say that when the Angel of Death told the story to God, the Holy One laughed aloud at the wisdom of the woman who reclaimed the soul of her husband from the hand of the Angel of Death.[2]

One way to put off the Angel of Death is through the birth of children, life lived on through kin and blood ties to the future. The blessings are passed on, along with the faith and trust in the God of the living, the God of Abraham, Isaac and Jacob, the God whose name is I AM WHO I AM, the God who is life, existence, being, all that is, was and will be.

There is another way too. The story is told in a Talmudic legend:

- Rabbi Joshua ben Levi loved the Torah. He spent hours bent over his books, studying, marveling at the Word of the Lord, blessed be his name. And one day, as he was immersed in study, the shadow of the Angel of Death fell across the page that he was touching reverently with his finger. Looking up, but without letting go of the text, the rabbi questioned the angel as to why he was there. The Angel of Death responded that it would soon be time for the rabbi.

Looking straight into the eyes of the Angel of Death, the rabbi asked a favor: Would it be possible for him to see the place that was reserved for him in Paradise before he actually got there? The Angel of Death was surprised at the rabbi's boldness, but he was in a good mood and agreed to let him come and see his place in heaven.

But the rabbi told the angel that he really didn't trust him. He wanted the Angel of Death's sword to keep until they had seen the place and returned. The Angel of Death laughed: "I keep my word," he said, "believe me." But he handed over his sword as pledge of his word and took the rabbi to the walls of heaven.

Rabbi Joshua peered over the wall into Paradise and with the sword held tightly in hand, he jumped out of the angel's grasp, over the wall and into heaven before the Angel of Death realized what he was doing. The angels went crazy, flying about, stirring up a din and commotion; no one had ever entered heaven that way before! What was the Holy One going to do?

The Almighty, blessed be his name, hushed the angels and stilled the noise and looked with a twinkle in his eye at Rabbi Joshua ben Levi and declared that he should have the seat that he had spied from his perch on the wall of heaven. Then, looking at the Angel of Death, who was standing there ashamed and looking a bit stupid, the Holy One laughed aloud and told Rabbi Joshua that he'd have to give the sword back to the Angel of Death, its rightful owner, since the work of this angel was necessary for the survival of the earth and human beings. This angel too did the will of God, though it was considered one of the harder works of the Almighty.

Then God turned and faced the angels of heaven and the souls of the just and declared: "What Joshua ben Levi has done is the work of the world, the work of creation, the work of the just: to seize the sword of violence and do away with death, any death that does not serve life and the will of God. In that action and work lies the salvation and hope of earth and all its children. It is one of the ways to see the face of God and live!" (adapted from *Ketubot* 77b)[3]

The Angel of Death must do his work, as we must do ours. And part of our work is learning to face the reality of death, as necessary. It is no easy reality to face. There is a Mexican story that many tellers delight in sharing. I have heard it told by Angeles Arrien and Doug Lipman, and I tell it myself. It speaks of truth and hope as well as leave-taking, living and dying.

- Once upon a time, there was a poor poor man, Antonio, and his beloved wife, Esperanza. They had eight children already and on the Feast of the Day of the Dead [November 2, Feast of All Souls] Esperanza gave birth to their ninth, a boy. What a blessing, to have a child born on the Day of the Dead, so closely tied to the ancestors and those who had gone before in faith! This child would be the turning point in their life, a blessing that would bring prosperity and security to their old age.

  But Antonio's immediate task was to find a *madrina* [godmother]. He must find a good one, with all the qualities he wished his new son to have: justice, mercy, truthtelling and power. But who? He thought of the wealthy señora who presided over the great hacienda where he worked. After all, she had power. But then again, he knew she was lacking in justice and mercy. What about one of the poor ones who worked the fields with him, one of the holy women trained in the lore of herbs and medicine? She would know justice and mercy—but she did not have power in the world. There is no power in poverty, as he already knew well. He went walking, wondering who would be the *madrina* of his newborn.

As he walked he was approached by a woman he did not recognize. She was tall, elegant and thin, wrapped in a long cloak that hid her face from him. She walked with grace and freedom, as one who is used to power and honor walks. She spoke forthrightly to Antonio, "I know you have a child, newborn, and you are looking for a *madrina* who can give him what he needs: justice, mercy, truthfulness and power. Let me be his *madrina*. I can give him this." "But who are you?" Antonio demanded. "I do not know you." She looked at him kindly. "Yes, you do, Antonio, I am *La Muerta* [Death]. Four times I have visited your house. You know me."

La Muerta! Yes, he decided quickly. She would be a perfect *madrina*, for she took the rich and the poor, practicing justice and mercy. There is no power on earth that can stand against her and she is, at the end, truthful. All stand before her without anything but their lives. Yes, she would make a great *madrina*. He was honored that she asked, and he turned for home knowing that *La Muerta* was as good as her word.

His son Julio grew in stature and grace, happy and carefree as a child. According to the custom, his *madrina*, *La Muerta*, appeared when he was of age to be taught. She took him into the woods and taught him all the herbs and medicines and wisdom that comes with healing and suffering. Soon he was wiser and surer of his profession than any in the land.

When his time of apprenticeship was over, she came to him once more, with a gift. She showed him a pale yellow flower, a flower that was often overlooked in the forest when it was seen, but often not seen when it was looked for. "This," she said, "is *la yerba de la vida*. If you make a medicine from this you can bring the dying back to life. But it has two properties that must be remembered, and you must follow my instructions carefully and without any disobedience. You and the one dying will see me. If you see me standing at the foot of the bed, then you may give the dying one the flower, *la yerba de la vida*. But if I am standing at the head of the bed, then you must not, for I have come to claim my own. It will be the person's time to die."

And so, Julio went into the world with all that his *madrina* had taught him. Soon many knew of him. He tended the rich and the poor equally. He worked with tenderness, strength, mercy and justice. His name became Julio de los Remedios. He cured many, and many also died. He would repeat the words of his *madrina*: "Sometimes it is kinder not to cure." To others he would say: "No, let go, death comes for this one and it is time."

One day the king of the land sent for him. The king had proclaimed that anyone who could save him from death would get half the kingdom as payment. As Julio de los Remedios traveled toward the king's great house he thought: Ah, this is it. This is my time. I will save the king from death. I will have half his kingdom, and my old parents will live out their last years with security and ease.

He took with him his pale yellow flower medicine, *la yerba de la vida*. He came straight into the king's bedchamber, but who should be standing at the head of the bed but his *madrina*, the tall, stately figure of *La Muerta*. He was stunned. This was not expected. He wanted half the kingdom for his parents and himself. He would cheat her, disobey her, just this one time. He shouted out to those standing around the bed: "Quick, the king needs fresh air— turn his bed so that his head is close to the windows." This was done in a flash, and *La Muerta* found herself standing at the foot of the king's bed. Quickly Julio gave the king the herb and the king stood up, healed, strong with life. All eyes

were on the king, all eyes except Julio's. He found himself
looking into the stern, dark eyes of his *madrina, La Muerta.*
She was not pleased and extended her long arm and finger
at him, saying, "You do that again and I will come for you
instead." The voice was cold, icy and adamant. Julio
blanched and nodded to his *madrina.*

Now Julio was rich and lived in the court of the king.
Oh, he still visited the hovels of the poor and the fields,
but he had learned to like the company of kings, princes
and nobles. Soon, one in particular won his heart: the
daughter of the king. A date for the wedding was set. Julio
could not believe his good fortune.

But a week before the wedding his beloved princess fell
ill. He was crushed with grief, for he saw her sliding toward
the shadows. But he remembered. He was Julio de los
Remedios. He would save her. Out into the woods he went
looking for the pale yellow flower *la yerba de la vida,* so hard
to find when you seek it. But Julio never failed, and with the
flowers clutched in his hand, he flew back to the princess's
room and quickly made the medicine. He approached her
with great tenderness and raised it to her lips.

But who should be standing at the head of the bed but
La Muerta, his *madrina.* No, he cried out in his heart. His
madrina, his beloved godmother, would not take his
beloved from him. She couldn't. And he thought, just one
more time I will disobey her. He turned the bed around
and fed the princess *la yerba de la vida,* and she sat up, her
shining eyes looking at him with love. But his eyes sought
La Muerta—would she take his life? There was no one
there. *La Muerta* was gone.

A week later, as planned, they were married. That night
he knew his beloved, and they slept in each other's arms,
full of joy. But after they had fallen to sleep a knock came
at the door. When he opened it, *La Muerta* was standing
there before him. She motioned, and he followed her out

into the night, outside the palace, the city, and onto the roads, following paths he had never seen before.

Finally they came to the mouth of a great cave and entered it. They walked in and down, deeper and deeper into the core of the earth, until at last they came to a great cavern full of light. In it were thousands upon thousands of candles burning bright. Some were new, others flickering, some half-spent, others just stubs in the sand. One would sputter out and another would burst forth. It was a dance, a fiery dance that was done in great silence.

Julio asked his *madrina*, "What is this place?" She answered, "These are the lights of people's lives."

Julio looked, his eyes drawn down to a small candle at his feet. It was nearly burned out. The wick had fallen over and it was sputtering in the hot melting wax. "Whose is that?" She looked at him and spoke softly, "That one, Julio, is yours."

"Mine?!" he cried out. "*Madrina*, have mercy on me. Let me live. I have only had one night with my beloved wife."

"But I have had mercy on you, great mercy—twice. I gave you mercy in the life of the king and again in the life of your wife. Now I give you mercy a third time." Her long finger extended again—to a large towering candle, solid and strong, the wick just flickering into flame. "There," she pointed, "that candle is your child, conceived this night! I have shown you great mercy."

But Julio begged and pleaded. "I am a father. Please, spare my life a little longer."

"No, Julio," she spoke. "I am your *madrina*. I told your father, Antonio, that I would give you what you needed: mercy, justice, truthfulness and power. I have already given you power and mercy. Now it is time for the justice and truth."

She looked at him with great sadness and great love. Then she took her eyes from Julio's face and, turning, bent over his candle and blew it out. Julio de los Remedios died that night.

Stories in every culture speak of the inevitability of death. But they also speak of the interconnectedness of all life, of the passing of life onto others. *La Muerta*, the Angel of Death, can be merciful and just, but also powerful and truthful, giving and taking. But the Angel of Death does not act on whim or fancy. There is meaning. Death can bond as surely, though radically differently, as life.

In the Christian tradition, Uriel, the Angel of Death, is not just the angel of final death, the letting go of life, but the angel of transformation and conversion, standing in our presence and letting his shadow fall over us whenever something in us needs to be let go of, turned aside from or died to. Christians are commissioned to deny our very self, pick up our cross and follow Jesus. The path leads to Jerusalem and to death, death on a cross and, of course, to resurrection. We are called to obedience and to trust in the meaning of suffering and death as the prelude to life and resurrection in the person of Jesus Christ. Paul's hymn in Philippians speaks of Jesus' acceptance of death:

> He humbled himself by being obedient to death,
> death on a cross.
> That is why God exalted him
> and gave him the Name which outshines all names,
> so that at the Name of Jesus all knees should bend
> in heaven, on earth and among the dead,
> and all tongues proclaim that Christ Jesus is the Lord
> to the glory of God the Father. (Phil. 2:8–11)

The Angel of Death came for Jesus on the cross, and Jesus freely handed over his life, saying, "Father, into your hands, I commend my spirit." Saying that, he gave up his spirit (Luke 23:46). But death could not hold him long. The Easter Vigil of the early church is rife with wild language about the freeing of Christ from death, the raising up of Jesus by his Father in resurrection.

In an Easter Sermon of St. John Chrysostom we read:

> No one need fear death; for our Savior
>   himself has died and set us free.
> He confronted death in his own person, and
>   blasted it to nothing.
> He made it defunct by the very taste of his flesh.
> This is exactly what Isaiah foretold when he declared:
> "Hell is harrowed by encounter with him."
>
> Of course it is harrowed.
> For now hell is a joke, finished, done with.
> Harrowed because now taken prisoner.
> It snatched a body and—incredible—lit upon God.
> It gulped down the earth, and gagged on heaven.
> It seized what it saw, and was crushed by what it failed
>   to see.
>
> Poor death, where is your sting?
> Poor hell, where is your triumph?
> Christ steps out of the tomb and you are reduced to
>   nothing.
> Christ rises and the angels are wild with delight.
> Christ rises and life is set free.
> Christ rises and the graves are emptied of dead.
> Oh yes, for he broke from the tomb like a flower, a beauti-
>   ful fruit: the first fruit of those already gone.
> All glory be his, all success and power…for ever and ever.[4]

The Angel of Death now serves the Lord of Life, and all those baptized into the death of Christ live "no longer for themselves alone, but they live hidden now, with Christ in God" (Easter liturgy). Now nothing, not even death, can deter us from life. Christians, Christ-bearers, light-bearers, can stand secure in opposition to death that is the result of sin, evil, injustice, violence and hate. Paul proclaims to the Philippians: "I want to know him: I want to experience the power of his resurrection and share in his sufferings and become like him in his death. May I attain the resurrection from the dead!" (3:10).

And it is not just human beings that know a taste of this life and freedom from death. In Romans, Paul says:

> All creation is eagerly expecting the transformation of the children of God. For the created world was subjected to frustration; this did not come from itself, but from the one who subjected it. But it is not without hope; for even the created world will be freed from this fate of death and share the freedom and Glory of the children of God.
>
> We know that the whole creation groans and suffers the pangs of birth. Not creation alone, but even ourselves, although the Spirit was given to us as a foretaste of what we are to receive, we groan in our innermost being, eagerly awaiting the day when God will adopt us and take to himself our bodies as well. (Rom. 8:19–23)

The Angel of Death in the new creation knows its limits and serves those who can face down death, even though they love life. Uriel is friend to the children of God and has been their shadow since baptism. Uriel is the angel of conversion, transformation and emptying out of one's self so that the Spirit of God can enter in and find a dwelling place. Uriel stands with those who oppose evil and those who oppose any form of death that does not come from the hand of the angel who obeys only the will of God. In fact, Uriel comes to those who again and again choose life, choose to be converted to the following of the way of the cross. As the German poet Rainer Maria Rilke says, "If the angel deigns to come it will be because you have convinced her, not by tears but by your humble resolve to be always beginning: to be a beginner."

Uriel is the angel of novices, those intent on and enthusiastic for the fullness of life and hope that is practiced all the way home to death and resurrection. Uriel is the angel of intense devotion, the protector and shadow of all who study life, preserve life and oppose unnatural death. Uriel stands with the other three who form the space before the throne of God, who is both justice and mercy, the giver of all life. Uriel claims us finally for Life, in death.

NOTES

1. Adapted from Moses Gaster, *Ma'aseh Book* (Philadelphia: Jewish Publication Society, 1934), 1:30.

2. One version of this folktale by Dov Noy was reprinted in *Moroccan Jewish Folktales* (New York: World Zionist Organization/ Herzl Press, 1966). Reprinted with permission.

3. Another version of this story can be found in Morris B. Margolies, *A Gathering of Angels: Angels in Jewish Life and Literature* (New York: Ballantine Books, 1994), pp. 143–44.

4. Translation by Paul Roche, *America* (April 5, 1980).

5

THE ANGEL OF RECIDIVISM

Recidivism, according to the dictionary, is "a tendency to relapse into a previous condition or mode of behavior, especially relapse into criminal behavior." It is characteristically recurring, habitual criminal action. And so, "the Angel of Recidivism," as Daniel Berrigan calls this angel, is the one who lures, the one who leads us into patterns that upset the social order and refuse to allow history to ignore the reality of truth according to the gospel.

The stories that give rise to the naming of this angel are found primarily in the Acts of the Apostles, chapters 5 and 12. In chapter 5, Peter meets with the believers in Jerusalem. People bring their sick to Solomon's portico hoping that Peter's shadow might fall on them. The high priest and his supporters, the Sadducees, become jealous of the apostles and have them arrested and thrown in the public jail. "But an angel of the Lord opened the door of the prison during the night, brought them out, and said to them, 'Go and stand in the Temple court and give the people the message of life.' Accordingly they entered the Temple at dawn and resumed their teaching." This kind of behavior is what got them landed in the clink in the first place!

The court convenes and the prisoners are sent for and the soldiers return with the report: "We found the prison securely locked and the prison guards at their post outside the gate, but when we opened the gate, we found no one inside." Everyone is baffled. Word spreads quickly, and the Sanhedrin is informed that the apostles are back at their preaching. They are brought back to court by the guards, this time without any show of force, to face the music. The charge is clear: "We gave you strict orders not to preach such a Savior; but you have filled Jerusalem with your teaching and you intend charging us with the killing of this man." The apostles' defense is crystal clear: "Better for us to obey God rather than men!"

Bedlam ensues but Gamaliel, a teacher of the Law, intervenes on the apostles' behalf and stills the murderers' intent for the time being. Gamaliel suggests that the prisoners be taken outside, and then he speaks to the assembly:

> "I advise you to have nothing to do with these men. Leave them alone. If their project or activity is of human origin, it will destroy itself. If, on the other hand, it is from God, you will not be able to destroy it and you may indeed find yourselves fighting against God." (Acts 5:38–39)

Gamaliel's speech persuades them; the council has the apostles whipped and orders them not to speak again of Jesus the Savior. Then, they set them free. The result of the sentencing? "The apostles went out from the Council rejoicing that they were considered worthy to suffer disgrace for the sake of the Name. Day after day, both in the Temple and in people's homes, they continued to teach and to proclaim that Jesus was the Messiah." Persistent, no doubt about it.

Persecution soon sets in. King Herod has James killed, and when he sees that doing so greatly pleases the Jews, he has Peter arrested also. Herod seizes him and throws him into prison to await a public trial. On the night before the trial, the Angel of Recidivism comes again—a bit of light intruding in the darkness.

> Peter was sleeping between two soldiers, bound by a double chain, while guards kept watch at the gate of the prison.
>
> Suddenly an angel of the Lord stood there and a light shone in the prison cell. The angel tapped Peter on the side

and woke him saying: "Get up quickly!" At once the chains fell from Peter's wrists. The angel said, "Put on your belt and your sandals." Peter did so, and the angel added, "Now, put on your cloak and follow me." [Peter has heard *those* commands before.]

Peter followed him out; yet he did not realize that what was happening to him with the angel was real; he thought he was seeing a vision. They passed the first guard and then the second and they came to the iron door leading out to the city, which opened of itself for them. They went out and made their way down a narrow alley, when suddenly the angel left him. [Angels have a disconcerting way of just disappearing, like the One they serve.]

Then Peter recovered his senses and said, "Now I know that the Lord has sent his angel and has rescued me from Herod's clutches and from all that the Jews had in store for me." Peter then found his bearings and came to the house of Mary, the mother of John also known as Mark, where many were gathered together and were praying. (Acts 12:6–12)

What follows reads like a comedy, with Mary so excited that she goes to announce the good news of his freedom and forgets to unlock the door; Peter is left waiting outside. At daybreak, the guards pay heavily for Herod's frustration: they are questioned and then executed. The pattern is set: preach about the power of the Name publicly; accuse evildoers of killing and injustice; get arrested, jailed, go to court, escape by the skin of the teeth (often losing some skin in the process); and go back and do it again. The Angel of Recidivism is loose and hard to ignore.

This angel seems to act as guardian spirit to those who stand in the breach and preach the presence and the power of that Name, that Name that cannot tolerate evil. Prophets are driven by the Angel of Recidivism. They know the hard realities and cannot abide easy avoidance of the issues. Not to describe insidiousness is to whitewash and contribute to the anguish it causes: decay unchecked, despair encouraged, hatred tolerated, unnecessary deaths forgotten, violence romanticized, pollution accommodated, spiritualities developed that desensitize the individual to the pain of others. These are the new rings of hell.

That Angel of Recidivism keeps commanding: go and give the people the message of life. 1 Peter reminds us that suffering and persecution are part of the gospel and that we shouldn't be surprised at the reaction of others to the proclamation of hope for sinners who repent.

> My dear people, do not be surprised that you are being tested by fire. It is not an unusual occurrence. Instead, you should be glad to share in the sufferings of Christ because, on the day his Glory is revealed, you will also fully rejoice. You are fortunate if you are insulted because of the name of Christ, for the Spirit of glory rests on you. I suppose that none of you should suffer for being a murderer, a thief, a criminal or an informer; but if anyone suffers on account of being a Christian, let him not be ashamed; rather let this name bring glory to God…. So, then, if you suffer according to God's will, entrust yourself to the faithful Creator and continue to do good. (1 Pet. 4:12–16, 19)

Eventually, obedience to the angel, obedience to Jesus, will lead to crucifixion. It was Jesus who told Peter, "Truly, I say to you, when you were young you put on your belt and walked where you liked. But when you grow old, you will stretch out your hands and another will put a belt around you and lead you where you do not wish to go." Jesus said this to make known the kind of death by which Peter was to glorify God. And he added, "Follow me" (John 21:18–19).

This angel is friend of jailbirds, hard-core "criminals" who obey the Word of God first and only obey the laws of a nation or government when they do not contradict the gospel.

The poet Denise Levertov has a marvelous poem entitled "St. Peter and the Angel." It tells of Peter's life after the angel left him.

And not till he saw that the angel
has left him,
alone and free to resume
the ecstatic, dangerous, wearisome
roads of
what he had still to do,
not till then did he recognize
this was no dream. More frightening
than arrest, than being chained to his warders:
he could hear his own footsteps suddenly.
Had the Angel's feet
made any sound? He could not recall.
No one had missed him, no one was in pursuit.
He himself must be the key, now, to the next door,
the next terrors of freedom and joy.

A visit from any angel leaves one disconcerted, drawn deeper into the mystery of God, deeper into the unknown ways of the kingdom of light coming inch by inch into this world, in spite of its resistance. The visit of every angel is terrifying.

Probably it was this Angel of Recidivism who came to Elijah when he was fleeing for his life from Jezebel, after slaying all her prophets of Baal. It was on the command of Elijah, not the command of God, that the false prophets were brought down to the Kidron brook and slaughtered by the people. Elijah was scared and fled for his life to Beer-sheba of Judah. He disappeared into the desert, traveling about a day's journey.

Then he sat down under a broom tree and prayed to die. "That is enough, Yahweh, take away my life for I am dying."
He lay down and went to sleep under the broom tree. Then an angel touched him and said, "Get up and eat."

Elijah looked and saw, at his head, a cake baked on hot stones and a jar of water. He ate and drank and went back to sleep. The angel of Yahweh came a second time to him, saying, "Get up and eat, for the journey is too long for you." He got up, ate and drank, and on the strength of that food, he traveled for forty days and forty nights to Horeb, the mount of God. (1 Kings 19:4–8)

That was some food!—much like the manna in the desert of Sinai. With it to eat, Elijah crossed the length of the two kingdoms of Israel and Judah. Elijah was going to encounter Yahweh on a solitary journey, with only an angel to sustain him with food and drink.

Elijah arrives at Horeb (Sinai), where Yahweh revealed his Name to Moses, four centuries earlier. Elijah must learn the heart of God. The image that expresses God best is the murmur of a gentle breeze, and Elijah perceives it. Yahweh sends him to anoint a king in Syria and another in Israel, and to throw his cloak over Elisha and anoint him as prophet in his place. Elijah has to learn the inner conversion of heart that he preached to the Israelites. He was the "disturber of Israel," but his work now is done. After the slaughter of the false prophets, an over-zealous personal reaction, Elijah passes on his ministry to Elisha at the command of God. Soon Yahweh will take Elijah up to heaven in a whirlwind with a chariot of fiery horses.

Thus the legend began that Elijah did not die but would return to prepare the people for the coming of the Messiah.

When Jesus began preaching, many in Israel believed he was the Messiah. John, in jail, sent word to Jesus, asking if he was the long-awaited one. Jail reduced even the prophet John to the bare essentials and tried his faith, in solitary confinement. John remained in jail, eventually to lose his head. He had to question and believe from a distance. Later Jesus warned his disciples:

"Be on your guard, for you will be arrested and taken to Jewish courts. You will be beaten in synagogues; and you will stand before governors and kings for my sake to bear witness before them. For all the nations must hear the preaching of the Gospel: this is the very beginning.

"So, when you are arrested and brought to trial, don't worry about what you are to say; but say whatever is given you in that hour. For it is not you who speak but the Holy Spirit.

"Brother will betray brother, even to death, and the father his child. Children will turn against their parents and have them put to death. And you will be hated by all for my name's sake. But whoever holds out to the end will be saved." (Mark 13:9–13)

This angel is the guardian of jails, patron of religious prisoners, those who practice civil disobedience, tell the truth to power and seek to protect the innocent with their words and lives laid on the line, always nonviolently. Perhaps the way the angels scratch on our souls these days is the scraping sound of sliding bars and prison doors, shackles dragging and the long-enduring days and nights of incarceration due to civil disobedience known in more scriptural communities as "preaching the Name." In some historical epochs and countries the angel is kept busy; in others this angel barely sees the inside of a jail, for those who call themselves Christians have grown easy with the powers of the world and learned to accommodate evil. When this angel languishes, the faith of Christians is weak-kneed and thin-spirited.

This angel reminds us that the usual boundaries of the natural world are slipping away, being eroded. Even though there is intent to harm those who belong to God and speak with the word of God in their mouths on behalf of others, the presence of the angel is a reminder that there is also blessing, freedom and hope given in the midst of torture, isolation and suffering. This angel is attracted by menace, oppression and the war between the powers of good and evil, always to the side of those favored by God in the conflict and facing terrible odds. The improbable message is always constant: Get up! Come! Get dressed: this place cannot hold you long and cannot contain or smother the zeal of your soul! It is time to go back to the work at hand: the preaching of life to the people!

In spite of long terms in jail, torture and inhumane treatment, those who know this angel know that in spite of what happens to their bodies and minds they are left with a blessing. This is the angel that Jacob reminds his children of: "May the God in whose presence my fathers Abraham and Isaac walked, the God who has been my shepherd from my birth to this day, the Angel who has saved me from every evil, bless these" (Gen. 48:15–16). This is the reference to the familiar psalm for funerals and hard times:

> Although I walk through the valley
> of the shadow of death,
> I fear no evil,
> for you are beside me.
> Your rod and your staff
> are there to comfort me.
> You prepare a table before me
> in the presence of my foes.
> You anoint my head with oil;
> my cup is overflowing.
> Goodness and kindness will follow me
> all the days of my life,
> I shall dwell in the house of the Lord
> as long as I live. (Ps. 23:4–6)

It is the Shepherd that sends the angel to those caught in the shadow for the honor of God and the life of the people.

This angel can come in the form of a human who shepherds the one in jail to freedom or in one who gives hope in the midst of the long trials. The angel inhabits the spaces where justice can be experienced, life can be lived and defended and promoted: these places are prerequisite for life for the poor and those in jeopardy, the majority of people in Latin America and other parts of the world. Phil McManus of the Fellowship of Reconciliation tells of Luis Perez Aguirre, a Jesuit who helped to found SERPAJ (*Servicio Paz y Justicia*) in Uruguay during the worst days of the military dictatorship (in the 1970s). It was his words, his educational methods and never-ceasing public testimony that caused him to be arrested and jailed. Now he is a special advisor on human rights to UN General Secretary Boutros Boutros-Ghali. McManus writes:

> He [Aguirre] lay nude in a completely dark cell. In between visits to his torturers, he discovered a message scratched by the fingernails of a previous prisoner on the wall of the cell. Using only his fingers, it was time-consuming to decipher it in the pitch black. But time was one thing he had. Gradually he was able to make out the greeting that brought light into his darkness: "All of the flowers of all of the tomorrows are found in the seeds of today."

The Angel of Recidivism does not always visit people in such extremities. Its presence can be experienced breaking boundaries and expanding limits that are much more mundane. I heard Eduardo Galeno tell this story in England, although a shortened version of it is found in *Genesis of Fire*, volume 1 of his three-volume history of Latin America:

- Once upon a time, a man was jailed for stealing food for his family in Mexico. Once a month his wife and child would come to visit him, bringing him food, clean clothes, something extra—cigarettes, candy, and so on. All month long the child, a young girl, thought about what to bring to her father, whom she missed and loved dearly. Finally she thought of all the times they had picked flowers together and walked in the forests and especially, times they had stopped and listened to the sound of the birds singing. She knew her father must miss the birds.

She drew a picture of the prettiest bird she had ever seen. Visiting day came and they both went to the prison: mother and daughter. They waited in line to pass through, with the guard checking through all their bags and bundles. When he came upon the picture, he asked what it was. Solemnly, she told him, "It is a bird, for my father." He looked at the list in his hand and abruptly tore up the picture, saying: "No, birds are not allowed in." She protested, saying, "But it's only a picture!" But it was torn to shreds and she went in empty-handed and silent.

For the next week, she was terribly unhappy. Then she decided to try again. This time she drew flowers, lots of them, all colors and shapes and sizes. The month was over, and again she and her mother waited in the line. The officer took one look at the picture and said: "No, no flowers are allowed." He tore up the picture. She was in tears but said nothing this time, and she once again had nothing to give to her beloved father.

Another month went by. She thought, What can I make him that will be allowed in? Finally she decided. She got a big piece of paper and colored it with brown and then on top of that all the other colors. It was finished. The officer in the line asked her what it was. "Just a picture," she said, taking it back from the officer. And she took it in with her, bursting with happiness. She couldn't wait to see her father. He unfolded it and looked at it and didn't know what to say. It was just a mess of colors and ragged lines. Finally, he looked at her with great affection and said: "It's lovely, *mi hija*, but what is it?" She looked very serious and said: "Oh, Papa, you know!" And then she explained to her bewildered father and mother. "Well, they wouldn't let the birds in or the flowers—he didn't know it was just a picture. So, this is a tree, a very thick tree with lots of leaves and the birds and the flowers are all hidden in there. But you and me, Papa, we know they're in there, don't we? If you look hard enough, you'll even be able to hear the singing of the birds." And the father held his child and wept.

Such are the disguises of the Angel of Recidivism.[1] They leave behind a trail of hope and steadfast resolve in the face of injustice and any power that would seek to make life inhuman or any space uninhabitable on this fair earth.

NOTE

1. My heartfelt thanks to Daniel Berrigan, who knows this Angel of Recidivism intimately.

6

ANGELS, LITURGY AND PRAYER

May I burst with jubilant praise to assenting angels.
— Rainer Maria Rilke

Many, many stories are told of angels and prayer. One is about the Ba'al Shem Tov, a rabbi.[1] It reminds all of us who pray what it is that we do when we call upon the Almighty and especially what we do when we pray together publicly in the rituals of liturgy and the seasons of the year.

- It was the holiest night of the Jewish year: Yom Kippur. The Ba'al Shem Tov was on his way to the synagogue to sing the Kol Nidre, the opening prayer. He was looking at his own life on this holy night and reflecting on his own sin. He thought sadly of all those that he had harmed, thought poorly of, ignored, was impatient with and had forgotten to pray for, after telling them that he would remember them to the Almighty, blest be his name. He thought of those he might have hurt carelessly with his fast retorts and public opinions and of all the times he had gotten angry and spoken harshly to those who needed a kind word or touch. He made mental lists of all the people he needed to ask forgiveness of on this night of conversion and forgiveness. He wanted to be prepared when he came before the Holy One, in the midst of all the people seeking to be restored to the arms of the Almighty and to have their names written in the book of the just. How could he ask for a year of blessing, a year of peace, before he remembered to forgive and to ask forgiveness humbly? Why, he knew that he had forgotten many things he had done or failed to do.

Now this was the holy man, the Ba'al Shem Tov, and he was concerned about the honor of God and his own unworthiness, and he was making his way slowly to the synagogue. He knew that not to know one's own sin and evil is dangerous, that to be unaware of one's sin is arrogant and stupid. He got close to the synagogue and realized it was full of people. Then, just as he got within a few feet of the open door, he stopped in his tracks. Right in front of him were angels or a vision of angels, as clear as the trees he had just passed through in the forest. There were multitudes of them, all hovering around the throne of God, and they were covering their ears with their hands and wings. They were shaking in terror and disappointment. He wondered what they were trying to block out. What sound was so bothering them that they were shaking? And then, he could hear what they were hearing and he froze. He couldn't believe his ears. Sound was coming out of the synagogue, which was so packed with people on this holy night when the children of Israel cry out for forgiveness and seek the mercy of God for breaking the covenant so often.

From the synagogue came words, falling over one another, the clamor of many people trying to be heard. It was a din of noise, a racket that grated on his ears and hurt them. The prayers of the people gathered in the synagogue were horrible! The people were selfish and greedy, thinking only of themselves and certainly not of God and his glory and holiness. They were not thinking of their sin or their need for forgiveness and reconciliation but of what they wanted God to do for them this night. The angels couldn't stand it and tried to cover their ears.

Just then some of the people noticed the Ba'al Shem Tov at the doorway and loudly welcomed him, inviting him in to pray with them. He didn't move and looked at them with horror. Finally, he found his voice and spoke: "I cannot come in," he said—"it's too crowded in there." The people looked around. It was crowded, but there was still room for him and probably a few more people. They could move over and make room, especially for the Ba'al Shem Tov. Again, they urged him to come and join them in their prayer. He looked hard at them and spoke again: "You have filled this place with your own sin and selfishness, your desires and your wants, not with prayer or the praise of the Almighty. There is nothing of repentance or cries for forgiveness. The place is full of horror. It is full of yourselves and not of the glory of God, the Holy One. I will not come in. There is no room for God or anyone who seeks God's face and mercy on this night. There is no room in the house of God for God to enter." And he turned on his heel and ran from the place, deep into the forest, covering his ears, like the angels, trying to drown out the din of human selfishness and sin. The Ba'al Shem Tov spent that Yom Kippur in the forest, with the angels, crying out for mercy for the children of God, sinners all.

Like the Ba'al Shem Tov, Isaiah the prophet was called by God to denounce the sins of the people and call them to true worship. The Book of Isaiah tells of the call of Isaiah the prophet. It is the year 740 BCE and Isaiah is in the Temple, or he sees himself there in the spirit. He is in the innermost part of the Temple, the place of the Ark of the Covenant, where only the Presence of God dwells, and he sees a vision of the Holy One. It is a vision of power and overflowing holiness, awe, terror and grace.

In the year that king Uzziah died I saw the Lord seated on a throne, high and exalted; the train of his robe filled the temple.

Above him were seraphs, each with six wings: two to cover the
face, two to cover the feet, and two to fly with.
They were calling to one another:
"Holy, holy, holy
is Yahweh Sabaoth.
All the earth is filled with his Glory!"

At the sound of their voices the foundations of the threshold
shook and the temple was filled with smoke. I said, "Poor me!
I am doomed! For I am a man of unclean lips living among a
people of unclean lips, and yet I have seen the King, Yahweh
Sabaoth."
Then one of the seraphs flew to me; in his hands was a live
coal which he had taken with tongs from the altar.
He touched my mouth with it and said,
"See, this has touched your lips;
your guilt is taken away
and your sin is forgiven."
Then I heard the voice of the Lord, "Whom shall I send?
And who will go for us?" I answered, "Here I am. Send me!"
He said, "Go and tell this people: 'Much as you hear, you
do not understand; much as you see, you do not perceive."
(Isa. 6:1–9)

Isaiah tells this vision from his past. This moment of encountering the holiness and mystery of God has marked him forever. It is
his call to mission; his call to announce to the people the anger and
displeasure of God and to denounce the people for their sacrifices
and works as an insult to God, not worship. This awareness of God
leaves him shaken and aware of his own sinfulness and unworthiness. It was commonly thought by the Israelites that to see God was
to die (Exod. 33:20). Being caught in the presence of God was
enough to take life and to stop the beating of one's heart. Isaiah is
terrified. The seraphim can survive the presence of God, but even

they must protect themselves from God's glory and the power that goes forth from God.

It is this acknowledgment of sin and his faith in the holiness of God that saves Isaiah from dying. One of the seraphim goes to him with a burning coal from the altar to sear his lips and purify him in body and soul so that he can stand in the presence of God and serve as God's prophet and respond to this question: "Whom shall I send?" Isaiah offers himself: "Send me!" The liturgy is complete. The word of God is spoken and taken to heart, heard. The offering of Isaiah's life is taken. His gift is transformed and he is sent out to proclaim the word of Yahweh to the people and the nations. That word goes forth with the power of God.

> As the rain and the snow come down
> from the heavens and do not return
> till they have watered the earth,
> making it yield seed for the sower
> and food for others to eat,
> so is my word that goes forth out of my mouth:
> it will not return to me idle,
> but it shall accomplish my will,
> the purpose for which it has been sent. (Isa. 55:10–11)

Isaiah's mission is to carry this glory of God out from the dwelling presence in the Temple into the hearts of the people, calling them to return to true worship and faithfulness to the covenant that they have scorned and laid aside for the worship of other gods. The people will harden their hearts and they will know ruin, but a root will spring from that barren desert that will blossom forth into a promise.

> Here is my servant whom I uphold,
> my chosen one in whom I delight.
> I have put my spirit upon him,

and he will bring justice to the nations.
He does not shout
or raise his voice in the streets.
A broken reed he will not crush,
nor will he snuff out the light
of the wavering wick.
He will make justice appear in truth.
He will not waver or be broken
until he has established justice on earth;
the islands are waiting for his law. (Isa. 42:1–4)

The words of Isaiah will come true in the person of the one who does justice with compassion and truth. The holiness of God will be his beloved servant and son, Jesus the Christ, the Holy One of God sent to save his people from their sins. The glory of God will be served by justice and truth. The glory of God will be in people who obey and do justice in the sight of God, laying down their lives so that others may know life. They will imitate Jesus, God become human and dwelling in our midst, his glory hidden in the least of our brothers and sisters.

This awareness of standing in the presence of the Lord and being in jeopardy of one's life is etched deep into the soul of the Jewish people. It is reflected in this story:

• A rabbi daily left home to go and pray in the Temple. But each morning when he took leave of his wife and child, he wept and clung to them and held them as if for the last time. When he was asked why he was so grief-stricken every morning he explained, "I go to stand before the presence of the living God and I call out to him to notice me, to hear my prayer. I begin with the ancient words of the shema: 'Hear, O Israel, the Lord your God is One.' What if the Almighty, blessed be his Name, should take heed of me and turn his face toward me? I am doomed, for I am a sinner, unholy, and would not be able to stand in God's presence. I would die and never see my beloved wife and children on this earth again. I must go from them each morning knowing that if I pray I may never see them again."

This is a startling tale and, for many of us who are familiar and all too accustomed to the presence of God and too unaware of our own sin, it may seem a bit far-fetched, an exaggeration. But if the presence and seeing of an angel puts fear and trembling into prophets like Daniel and Isaiah, what must a glimpse of the glory of God do to human beings!

Angels know about standing in the presence of God. Angels have been connected intimately with public worship and liturgy in the Temple and in the church from the beginning. The worship of God on earth is bound with the worship of God in the heavens. They reflect each other somehow. In the daily liturgy of the Eucharist the people of God join with the angels in prayer, lending their voices to the greater choir of the heavenly hosts. The early Fathers of the Church, especially John Chrysostom, declared that the Gloria is the prayer of the lower choirs of angels and so even the catechumens, those preparing for entrance into the mysteries of the Church, could sing that song together with all those who believe. But the Sanctus—the Holy, Holy, Holy—is the prayer of the highest choirs of angels, the seraphim, and so the catechumens had to leave before it. Only with the sacraments of initiation—baptism, confirmation and Eucharist—would they be privileged to sing with the angels that song of delight and wonder in the presence of the risen Lord.

The first part of the Eucharistic Prayer is called the prayer of warning, the preface, the prayer before the face of the Holy One. It cries out the presence of mystery, glory and power and then invites the community to sing its prayer with the thrones and dominations, the cherubim and the seraphim, because this prayer is the angelic prayer, the thrice-holy prayer to the Trinity. John Chrysostom says:

Reflect upon whom it is that you are near and with whom you are about to invoke God—the Cherubim. Think of the choirs you are about to enter. Let no one have any thought of earth (*sursum corda*), but let him lose himself of every earthly thing and transport himself whole and entire into heaven. Let him abide there beside the very throne of glory, hovering with the Seraphim, and singing the most holy song of the God of glory and majesty.[2]

In the first Eucharistic Prayer of the Roman liturgy, in its earliest form, it is the Angel of God who brings the gifts from the altar of earth to the altar of heaven: "May these gifts be brought by the hands of your holy angel to your altar on high." The angel is the bridge between heaven and earth, the bearer of our gifts of bread and wine, the one who returns with the gift transformed into the body and blood of Jesus Christ.

The early teachers of the Church are sure of the presence of the angels at liturgy. These angels are praying with us and they intercede for us, offering our prayers with the prayers of the saints and their own. Chrysostom writes:

It is not only men who raise this cry filled with holy awe, but the angels prostrate themselves before the Lord, the archangels pray to Him. Just as men cut palm branches and wave them before their kings to move them to think of love and mercy, so at this moment the angels present the very Body of their Lord as if it were a palm branch and they pray to Him for all humanity. (p. 65)

In fact, the teachers of the early Church often describe the angels as participating in the various liturgical seasons and celebrations of the Church, rejoicing with us over the great works of God in Jesus Christ. Describing the Feast of the Epiphany, the showing forth of the glory of God to the nations, Gregory Nazianzen writes:

Together with the shepherds glorify God; sing His praises with the angels; join the choirs of the archangels. Let this festive occasion join the powers of those in heaven and those on earth. For I am certain that they are rejoicing today and celebrating this feast together with us, since they are friends of God and man just as those whom David shows us rising with Christ after the Passion, going on ahead of Him and vying with each other to lift up the gates. (p. 65)

This role of praising and worshiping God without ceasing seems to be a primary reason for the existence of angels; it is what they do continuously. It is their nature to acknowledge and praise God. They are adept at devotion and veneration, worship and adoration. In the Book of Revelation, John describes a vision of the future, of heaven.

> I went on looking; I heard the noise of a multitude of angels gathered around the throne, the living creatures and the elders, numbering millions of millions, crying out with a loud voice:
> Worthy is the Lamb who was slain to receive
> power and riches, wisdom and strength,
> honor, glory and praise. (Rev. 5:11–12)

This has been their work, the essence of their existence since before history. Psalm 148 cries out:

> Alleluia! Praise the Lord from the heavens;
> praise him in the heavenly heights.
> Praise him, all his angels; praise him,
> all his heavenly hosts....
> For his name alone is exalted; his majesty is above earth and
> heaven and he has given his people glory.
> This is his praise from his faithful, from the children of
> Israel, the people close to him. Alleluia. (Ps. 148:1–2,
> 13–14)

The last line implies that it is the work and delight of the people close to God to praise and to stand in the divine presence and serve God. God delights in the songs and prayers of the angels, but all the stories and tales of earth seek to remind us that God also delights in the prayers and songs of certain unlikely souls on earth that somehow are more dear to him and dwell in his presence— though oftentimes unaware of his nearness and glory because of their unself-conscious devotion, love and humility. It seems there are some prayers that the Holy One yearns to hear from below!

And he will summon all the forces of the heavens, and all the holy ones above, and the forces of the Lord—the cherubim, seraphim, ophanim, all the angels of governance, the Elect One, and the other forces on earth (and) over the water. On that day, they shall lift up in one voice, blessing, glorifying, and extolling in the spirit of faith, in the spirit of wisdom and patience, in the spirit of mercy, in the spirit of justice and peace, and in the spirit of generosity. They shall all say in one voice, "Blessed (is he) and may the name of the Lord of the Spirits be blessed forever and evermore." All the vigilant ones in heaven above shall bless him; all the holy ones who are in heaven shall bless him; all the elect ones who dwell in the garden of life (shall bless him); every spirit of light that is capable of blessing, glorifying, extolling, and sanctifying your blessed name (shall bless him); and all flesh shall glorify and bless your name with an exceedingly limitless power forever and ever. (1 Enoch 61:10–12)

There is an old Jewish story told in Spain (and also in northern New Mexico) about a simple shepherd.

- Once upon a time, there was a poor man who was a shepherd. He would go to church on the high holy days if he could get someone to take care of his sheep. But he missed the Sabbath a lot when he couldn't go to the synagogue. A

simple man who didn't know how to read or write, he
spent a great deal of time in the fields with just his sheep
for company.

But he really loved God and so he prayed a lot in the
fields and he made up his prayers as he went along. He'd
be out in the fields in all kinds of weather with the sheep,
and at the top of his lungs he'd shout out, "O God, if you
had sheep I'd take care of them for free. Everybody else, I'd
charge, I'd charge them a lot, but for you, because I love
you so much, I'd keep your sheep for free." And then he
might rest for a few minutes, and then he'd say, "O God,
if I had radishes I'd give you half of my radishes because I
love radishes so much. But if you were still hungry, I'd give
you all of my radishes because that's how much I love you!"

And he would wander off to make sure the sheep
weren't getting lost and then he'd start again, "O God, if it
was raining and if you were getting wet, I'd give you my
hat if you didn't have one. And if you were still getting wet,
I'd give you my cloak and if you were still getting wet, I'd
hover over you and the rain could fall on me instead of you
because that's how much I love you!"

Well, this went on day after day, night after night, as the
shepherd prayed at the top of his lungs. The months went
by and the years went by and one day a rabbi, on his way
to the synagogue in town for the high holy days, was running late and decided to cut across the fields. When he was
halfway across the fields to the place where all the sheep
were gathered he heard someone yelling, at the top of his
lungs, "O God, if I had radishes, I'd give you half of my
radishes! I love radishes so much but if you were still hungry, I'd give you all of my radishes because that's how much
I love you!"

And the rabbi exclaimed, "What in the world is going
on?!"

And he continued across the field and he heard the next part. "O God, if it were raining and you didn't have a house, I'd give you my hat. O God, if you were still getting wet, I'd give you my cloak. O God, if you were still getting wet, I'd hover over you and let the rain fall on me instead of you because that's how much I love you!"

By now the rabbi was quite close to the shepherd. He saw him and called out, "What are you doing?"

"I'm praying," replied the shepherd.

"You're what? You call that kind of twaddling, that kind of screaming at the top of your lungs, praying? Who taught you that?"

"Well, nobody," said the shepherd. "I never really learned how to pray so I just make it up as I go along."

The rabbi said, "That's the stupidest prayer I've ever heard! The Almighty, blessed be his Name, the Maker and Creator of the universe, doesn't need your hat, doesn't need your cloak, doesn't get wet. He made the rain. He made the clouds. He made the earth. That's the stupidest prayer I've ever heard."

The poor shepherd was so ashamed. He stood there with his head hanging. The rabbi said, "Listen, I have to go to the synagogue for the high holy days and I'm already running late but I'm going to take some time out to teach you how to pray."

So the shepherd went over by the rabbi and the rabbi told him to repeat after him the morning prayer. He did the basics, line by line, and the shepherd very carefully repeated it, line by line. Then the rabbi instructed him to say this prayer at a certain time in the morning and when the sun is high to repeat another prayer and a third prayer for when the sun goes down. The rabbi then told him, "I don't want to hear you praying again the way you were before. If you don't remember how to pray correctly, then don't pray at all." And the rabbi rushed off to the synagogue.

The shepherd went back to his sheep. He realized he didn't understand a single thing the rabbi had told him. He didn't remember any of it. He had repeated it by rote but because he didn't understand a word he couldn't remember. He felt so ashamed and so humiliated to not remember the prayers that he just gave up. He didn't pray any more.

Now there was a curious silence in the fields with just the soft sound of the sheep. The shepherd quietly watched the sheep in the fields, and God, blessed be his Name, whose kingdom people think is way high in the heavens but who is very near to everyone on earth, instantaneously knew that something was desperately wrong. God listened. He listened to the whole world. He could hear the crickets and the blades of grass. He could hear the fireflies flickering. He heard every second and every bird's sound as it flew off. He listened to the sighs of lovers as they walked down the lane. He listened to the breathing of children as they dropped off to sleep. He even heard the spiders weaving webs in corners. He knew something was missing but he just couldn't quite put his finger on it. And then it hit him. "Radishes! The shepherd is not yelling at me about the radishes! He's not offering me his radishes or his hat. Something is terribly wrong with the shepherd. Gabriel! Raphael! Come here! You have to go down. You have to go and see what's wrong with the shepherd. He's not yelling about his radishes to me and he's not telling me how much he loves me. You must go down and help him."

So Gabriel and Raphael swooped down and landed in the fields. The shepherd was so forlorn that at first even the angels didn't catch his attention. Then his eyes opened up wide. Gabriel spoke first, "Why aren't you praying?"

The shepherd said, "I'm too ashamed."

Raphael asked, "Why? God misses your prayer. Why aren't you praying?"

"The rabbi told me not to," replied the shepherd. "He said what I was saying was twaddle and yelling at the Almighty and that the Almighty doesn't need my hat, that he doesn't want my radishes."

"But what in the world does a rabbi know about praying?" asked Gabriel.

"I would think a rabbi would know everything," said the shepherd.

"The rabbi doesn't know anything," said Raphael. "After all, does the rabbi know how the angels in heaven pray? How the cherubim and the seraphim, the thrones and dominations and powers, the virtues and archangels and angels pray?"

"I don't know," said the shepherd. "How do they pray?"

Gabriel looked at the shepherd and said, "They pray just like you."

"Really? What? No! Could I hear the angels praising God in all their harmony?"

Gabriel looked at Raphael and said, "Why not?"

And so they swooped down, put their arms around him and lifted him up, and off they went out of the fields and through the sky, past the clouds and way up past the stars and they came right to the edge of the gates of heaven. And they told the shepherd that he couldn't go any farther but to be quiet and listen.

And then they started, the seraphim and the cherubim on one side, "O God, if I had radishes." And on the other side the thrones and the dominations sang forth, "I'd give you half!" The first side continued, "If you were hungry," and the second side responded, "I'd give you all of them." And together in chorus, "That's how much we love you."

And the shepherd said to himself, "They really do pray just like me."

Gabriel said, "Yes, that's the only way to pray. You are supposed to pray with a simple, pure heart about everything that's important to you. Forget what the rabbi said."

And so they put their wings over him again and back they flew through the universe, past the stars, down through the clouds, and back to the fields of sheep. And the last thing that Gabriel and Raphael heard as they set off home, "O God, if I had radishes I'd give you half and if you were still hungry...." And an echo came back from heaven, "I'd give you all my radishes!" sang the angels. All together the shepherd and the angels sang the chorus, "That's how much I love you! That's how much I love you! That's how much I love you!"

The angels, wise in their world, recognize the wisdom of this world long before some of us who dwell here do. Perhaps even angels can learn from a person with a pure heart, a person who really loves God. Perhaps.

NOTES

1. I first heard this version from Rabbi Shlomo Carlebach in a synagogue in New York City.

2. John Chrysostom, quoted in Jean Daniélou, S.J., *The Angels and Their Mission: According to the Fathers of the Church* (Westminster, MD: Christian Classics, 1953), 64.

7
───────

ANGELS AND HOSPITALITY

Our Guardian Angels

*Do not neglect to offer hospitality; you know that some
people have entertained angels without knowing it.*
— Hebrews 13:2

*For an angel of peace, a faithful guide, a guardian of our
souls and bodies, let us entreat the Lord.*
— From a litany of the Eastern Orthodox Church

When I was very small, my Nana would say: "Be careful what you
say. You never know when you might be speaking to an angel." I
would laugh or wonder, and I went through a period of time when
I watched people very closely to see if they were indeed angels. But
I didn't know exactly what I was looking for and so soon tired of
the exercise and took people more at face value. Then, when I was
about twenty-four, I heard a marvelous story that set me to wondering once again. It was a medieval morality tale told from the
point of view of an old, old woman remembering a time long past.
It began with the words my Nana had used with me:

- Be careful what you say. You never know when you might
  be speaking to an angel. It seems so long ago now. When I
  remember that time, I wonder if I imagined it all. But as I
  think on it, it all comes back so clearly. He was a king. If

───────
105

only I had known that at the time. But that is what the story is all about. I was young and full of dreams and hopes, and I wanted to better my position. I was a shepherd girl and spent most of the year in the high pastures tending my father's flocks. But I didn't intend to stay there always. I intended to marry above my station in life. Indeed, I had already received an offer from a tradesman in the village.

The king was looking for a wife, and he had seen me in the fields while he was out hunting. I had not seen him. I was busy daydreaming and planning my future life. The king did not want to be married because he was the king, however; he wanted the woman he would marry to choose him freely. So one day, he dressed himself in peasant clothes and set out for the fields where I was with my sheep. He laid aside his kingdom for a while and instructed his courtiers to meet him in the field in two weeks' time with two horses and clothes for a maiden. But I didn't know any of that.

He arrived late one afternoon. He said he was coming back from a long journey and would soon be home. He talked of far-off places and things I'd only dreamed about. He could read, and late in the day we would sit by the stream in the cool of shade and he would read to me: poetry, history, geography, philosophy. He was so excited about knowledge—anything that told him of life and the world I considered to be far beyond my domain. The time passed quickly, and he asked me to marry him. We had talked of family and children and the future, and I had told him that I had already had offers from the tradesmen of the village and that I didn't always want to be just a shepherd's daughter. I wanted more than that and he told me that he could give me more than my heart's desire.

But how could I know? He was dressed as a traveler. He was a stranger to me, almost foreign in his ways of talking and thinking. Then one day he said, "You must decide soon, for I must be on my way."

That day was so long. I cared about him, but I cared more for my position in life and the sure position that I had already been offered. His offer was full of mystery, of hopes and trust. We sat at the edge of the field, and I finally told him, "I'm sorry, I cannot go with you."

He looked at me so strangely and said, "Can you not trust me?"

"No," I said, "I cannot."

He rose before me. He had seen them coming—his courtiers and the horses. I stood up too and they approached him, calling him king. My heart fell. What had I done in my lack of trust of this good man who made my heart ache and dream, but whom I could not trust? He mounted his horse and told them that the other horse and clothes would not be needed. I watched him ride away. He never looked back.

But it was so long ago and so much fades in my memory, all but his face when he asked me that question: "Can you not trust me?" I wonder often what my life would have been like if I had trusted that stranger so long ago. I never married. I still tend the sheep and live alone high in the mountain valleys and wonder if he ever sees me, still. If only I had remembered what my grandmother had told me: "Be careful. You never know when you might be speaking to an angel." I wonder if I will ever see him again, for I have lived with him ever since and learned hope. It was so hard to learn this way. I wonder too if now, after all these years, I have learned trust.

The story is sad, full of wisdom learned the hard way through experience, mistakes, regret, even remorse. And it has a finality to it, a sense that some things are lost forever in the decision and words of a moment. Angels have that kind of effect, especially if we miss their meaning, their presence or fail their questioning. Angels and strangers both question us and our deepest assumptions; they call us to risk, to hope and to trust. Theirs is not a lesson we learn easily.

There are stories of such visits by strangers—angels—in the Bible. In the Book of Genesis God comes to visit Abraham in the form of three men. This picture of Abraham entertaining three men, three angels, the presence of God, is famous. It is the basis of paintings by Chagall and the subject of many icons in the Eastern Church and part of the basis for the doctrine of the Trinity. It begins simply enough, with travelers being welcomed, as was the custom of the desert dwellers.

> Yahweh appeared to Abraham near the oak of Mamre. Abraham was sitting at the entrance to his tent, in the heat of the day, when he looked up and saw three men standing nearby. When he saw them he ran from the entrance of the tent to meet them. He bowed to the ground and said, "My Lord, if I have found favor in your sight, do not pass your servant by. Let a little water be brought. Wash your feet and then rest under the trees. I shall fetch some bread so that you can be refreshed and continue on your way, since you have come to your servant." They then said, "Do as you say." Abraham hurried into the tent to Sarah and said to her: "Quick, take three measures of flour, knead it and make cakes."
>
> Abraham then ran to the herd, took a fine, tender calf, and gave it to the servant who hurried to prepare it. He took butter and milk and together with the calf he had prepared, laid it all before them. And while he remained standing, they ate. They then asked, "Where is Sarah, your wife?" Abraham answered, "She is in the tent." And the visitor said, "At this same time next year I will return and Sarah by then will have a son." (Gen. 18:1–10)

The rites of hospitality in the desert are demanding. To break or ignore them is the highest insult, and is even dangerous to members of communities that rely on others as they travel. For three days, strangers and visitors must be given food and drink, water, bathing facilities and clean garments and a place to rest. Only then may they be sent on their way, refreshed and strengthened for their journey in the desert. Hospitality is held in high regard and esteem even today in Bedouin countries and cultures.

The story of Abraham's visitors reminds all those who meet strangers to be careful; we can entertain angels unawares and even find ourselves in the presence of the Lord of hosts in human form visiting the earth.

Abraham is gracious and generous in his hospitality, picking out the food and waiting on the guests himself. They, in turn, have been sent to deliver news: Sarah will have a child within the year. Some would say it is a blessing in response to the hospitality of Abraham and Sarah. God responds to their openhandedness with equal generosity: a child in their old age to care for them in their need, a link to the future, hope and fulfillment of the promise that God has already made to Abraham in the covenant (Gen. 15, 17).

But Sarah is behind Abraham in the tent, listening, and when she hears the good tidings she laughs to herself. Such a thing was unlikely if not impossible at her age. And Yahweh, one of the three visitors, asks, "Why did Sarah laugh, saying: 'Am I really going to have a child now that I am old?' Is there anything that is impossible for God? At this same time next year I will return and Sarah by then will have a son." It is announced, declared and it will be. Sarah denies her laughter, afraid in their presence and knowledge. "But," he said, "you did laugh" (Gen. 18:13ff.). Later Sarah herself will declare: "God has brought me laughter and everyone who hears of this will laugh with me." Isaac, her child's name, means "and she laughed." Abraham was a hundred, Sarah, not far behind him in age.

In the early books of the Bible sometimes the angel is the messenger of God, sometimes accompanies the presence of God, and sometimes is the image of God in a form that can be tolerated by human sight and mind. In this portion of Genesis Yahweh God is one of the three "men" that come to the tent, the one that does the speaking to both Abraham and Sarah. As the story continues, the men set off on the road to Sodom, and Abraham walks with them to set them in the right direction. Yahweh takes Abraham into his confidence on what he intends to do to the inhabitants of Sodom. He plans to do justice, having judged them and seen their evil deeds and intent. He speaks clearly:

> "How great is the cry for justice against Sodom and Gomorrah! And how grievous is their sin! I am going down to see if they have done all that they are charged with in the outcry that has reached me. If it is not so, I will know."
> The men with him turned away and went towards Sodom, but Yahweh remained standing before Abraham. (Gen. 18:20–21)

Abraham, in the company of the Lord, grows bold and intervenes on behalf of the just in the city.

> "Will you really let the just perish with the wicked? Perhaps there are fifty good people in the town. Are you really going to let them perish? Would you not spare the place for the sake of these fifty righteous people? It would not be at all like you to do such a thing and you can't let the good perish with the wicked, nor treat the good and the wicked alike. Far be it from you! Will not the judge of all the earth be just?" Yahweh said, "If I find fifty good people in Sodom, I will spare the whole place for their sake." (Gen. 18:23–26)

Hospitality with Abraham overlaps into care for the good and righteous of a city. And in equal measure, the hospitality of Yahweh overflows into mercy, sparing the evil if there are fifty just people in the whole city. But once he has gotten started, Abraham continues to push his argument. Perhaps there will be only five less than fifty, or forty, or thirty, or twenty—for their sake will you spare the city? What about just ten? Obviously the city's reputation is beyond poor—only ten good people in a whole city! And yet Yahweh leaves Abraham with such a deal—for the sake of the ten, Yahweh will spare the whole city. And Abraham goes home. Hospitality has been extended far beyond the limits of his tent.

Hospitality and justice are the trademarks of a faithful person; one who follows the lead of God in both justice and mercy upon the people of the earth. Good and evil are acknowledged and judged rightly, but for the sake of the few good, the evil are spared, given a chance to change. God is friends with Abraham, taking him into his confidence, sharing his plans for portions of the human race that offend him, as well as assuring Abraham of the outcome of the covenant he has already established with Abraham and his descendants forever. Abraham can argue boldly with God, pleading on behalf of others, since he himself has already known a taste of the mercy and goodness of this God who has made a covenant with him.

The angels, the other two who were companions with Yahweh, continued alone to the city of Sodom.

> When the two angels reached Sodom in the evening, Lot was sitting at the gate of the town. As soon as he saw them, he rose to greet them, bowed his face to the ground, and said, "My lords, I pray you come to your servant's house to stay the night. Wash your feet, and then in the morning you may rise early and go on your way." They said, "No, we will spend the night in the square." But so strongly did he insist that they went with him to his house; there he prepared a meal for them, baking bread without yeast. This they ate. (Gen. 19:1–3)

Once again the angels are offered hospitality, though they intended to spend the night in the public square, as was the custom for travelers without relatives. The quality of hospitality toward strangers is at the root of human dignity, at the root of what it means to be human itself. Just as the prophets forcibly will remind the Israelite kings and people that the way they treat the widow, the orphan, the stranger and the alien in their midst reveals whether or not they are faithful to the covenant of their ancestors, this story points out the importance and necessity of welcoming the stranger and caring for the basic needs of all human beings. The two angels are taken into Lot's house. Lot had earlier parted from Abraham's family, slaves and servants because between them and their herds there was not enough water and grass. They had parted on good terms. Lot extends hospitality to the strangers. Perhaps, it is said, he was a righteous man, waiting at the gate to take travelers in, because he knew how strangers were treated in the city.

This story is told in the part of Genesis that is still very close to the spread of evil across the earth, when Noah is saved with just his family and the animals and other creatures of the earth. Earlier, the state of the earth and its inhabitants was described: "Yahweh saw how great was the wickedness of man on the earth and that evil was always the only thought of his heart. Yahweh regretted having created man on the earth and his heart grieved" (Gen. 6:5–6). But for the sake of Noah, who is pleasing to God, creation is not utterly destroyed. Now, for the sake of ten good people, perhaps the city of Sodom will not be destroyed. Evil still grieves the heart of God at the time of Abraham.

The angels have not yet gone to bed for the night when the townspeople gather outside the door of Lot's house, all the men of Sodom, young and old, intent on humiliating and dishonoring the strangers. Lot is also still considered a foreigner, new to the city, a man from afar, alien to their ways. The basic sin of Sodom is disrespect for guests, inhospitality to strangers, treating unjustly those in precarious situations away from home. All strangers and travelers must be welcomed and treated as angels of God. The very presence of aliens in our midst is a moment of judgment, a time of testing to reveal our humanness or inhumanity. The specific form of dishonoring in this story is not sexual; it is violence, rape and humiliation not based on any relationship. It is brutality.

Lot is desperate and goes out to reason with the people, shutting the door behind him, in an attempt to protect the two strangers he has taken responsibility for, now threatened by a mob. He even offers them his own two daughters rather than the two guests who are sheltered under his roof! But it is a violent situation, and violence always escalates in response to reasoning. It is not concerned with logic or rational thinking or behavior but is based on evil and irrational desires.

The two angels drag Lot back in, away from the mob, and the members of the mob closest to the door of the house are struck blind and unable to find the door. The angels plead with Lot to take his family and household and get out of the place. They announce that they have been sent by God to destroy the city.

Lot tells his future sons-in-law what the two men intend to do, but they laugh and think it is just a joke. It seems they are not much better than the men of the town.

They make it through the night, and in the morning the angels urge Lot to take just his wife and two daughters and flee so that they will not perish on account of the sin of the city. Yahweh has had mercy on Lot and his family. They are told to run, not to look back and not to stop anywhere in the plain (Gen. 19:6–17).

But Lot doesn't think he can make it that far and asks for refuge in a small city, the town of Zoar, where he will be safe. He is granted his request. That town will not be destroyed. Again they are urged to flee because the angels cannot proceed until Lot's family arrives at a place of safety. The angels are obeying the will of Yahweh, sparing the good people before taking action and destroying the evil. There are only four good people in the town, it seems.

Destruction is fast and complete. Burning sulphur is rained down on the cities of Sodom and Gomorrah and all the land in between, the inhabitants and all growing things are wiped out.

Historically, these two cities were destroyed by earthquakes and the destruction completed by the overflow of salt and silt from the Red Sea. Forever afterward the prophets, even Jesus, will refer to these cities and their inhabitants when those to whom they preach conversion and repentance refuse to hear or to turn from their injustice and inhumanity to one another. The cities have become a symbol of evil, of the insensitivity that sin breeds in human beings as well as the perversity of even the basic relationships of men and women and hospitality as a basis for living on earth.

The story is problematic for modern readers. The judgment and swift destruction are based on one situation that results in all being judged and punished without recourse. Equally horrible is Lot's suggestion that they take his own daughters instead of his guests. And the ridicule of his future sons-in-law in the face of Lot's concern for both his guests and his family reveals the extent of the breakdown in familial relationships. All this reveals the pervasiveness of evil and its connection to violence, which is answered with destruction. On the other hand, hospitality is shown to be even more basic to a community's well-being than family ties. Justice is for all, especially the stranger and for those in dangerous situations. Angels take the guise and form of travelers, strangers, aliens, those in jeopardy racially, ethnically, even religiously. In those situations the foundations of society and justice are most clearly experienced or betrayed. This is basic undeniable good and evil, the underpinnings of society and the human race. Inhospitality, especially to the poor, the stranger, is inhospitality to the angels and to God. It merits swift justice and retribution. What was intended for the stranger is meted out by God to those who are already inhuman and evil.

Strangers come bearing gifts such as hope for the future, a line of descendants for those who believe in and respect the covenant of God, and laughter, impossible promises that do come true. Or they can come bearing judgment and retribution, revealing evil and calling forth the hatred and violence of human beings who prey upon the weak. We reveal what we are in the presence of strangers and in the rituals of hospitality. This will find new depth of meaning in how the human race treats the presence of the Holy One in a human being, a child born in Bethlehem of poor parents, in occupied territory among strangers. This child will preach hospitality to the poor, the blind, the deaf, the leper, the Samaritan, the exile, the slave, the enemy as criteria for entrance into the hospitality of the kingdom of God, even on earth. What we do to the "least" of our brothers and sisters is the criterion for judgment in this life and the next. It will reveal whether we are sheep or goats, children of the living, welcoming God or selfish individuals violent in our living and intent only on our own desires.

The passion accounts describe the horror of what happens when the Holy One falls into our hands and we deliver him up to death. That experience of the Suffering Servant, the Lamb of God, is no different from the experience of countless millions of the poor, the tortured, victims of war, prisoners and those without land, home and a place to rest on their journeys—all those who know violence and inhospitality as the mark of many human encounters devoid of God. Even in our own homes and places of worship we often miss the presence of the angels, disguised as they are in very ordinary forms, often in the forms of the slow, the sick, the feeble, those without the usual abilities and skills of the rest of the human race. Sometimes they are called retarded, bent, without sense, the innocent or, as Morris West names them, the clowns of God. They do not share the twistedness of many thought of as "normal."

The basis for what we call guardian angels is found in Matthew's gospel. It is in the portion of text concerned with scandals and who is greatest in the kingdom of heaven. Jesus takes a child and sets him in front of his disciples and tells them:

> "I assure you that unless you change and become like little children, you cannot enter the kingdom of Heaven. Whoever makes himself like this child is the greatest in the kingdom of

Heaven, and whoever receives such a child in my name receives me....

"See that you do not despise any of these little ones, for I tell you: their angels in Heaven continually see the face of my heavenly Father." (Matt. 18:3–5, 10)

The term "little ones" refers to more than just children. It refers to anyone without power in the dominant culture, much as sociologists refer to the Third World as all those countries and pockets of people in other countries that do not have access to resources, education, medicine, homes or other essentials of basic well-being. They are the ones "without," forgotten, lost, considered expendable, useless, problematic within a society based on usefulness, productivity and profit. Jesus is using a child to speak about slaves, servants, outsiders, foreigners, enemies even. He is emphasizing the necessity for his disciples to be careful in the presence of all these people, not to scandalize them. Jesus has just gotten through telling them in radical terms about the effects and consequences of sin: it is better to enter heaven maimed and destroyed than to enter eternal fire whole in limb and body. His sermon impresses upon us the horror of sin and its effect on those around us, especially those we never consider or even care if they witness our behavior.

The phrase about the little ones and their angels in heaven continually seeing the face of Jesus' heavenly Father is also the bridge to the short parable that follows immediately:

"What do you think of this? If a man has a hundred sheep and one of them strays, will he not leave the ninety-nine on the hills to go and look for the stray one? And I tell you: when he finally finds it, he is more pleased about it than about the ninety-nine that did not get lost. For your heavenly Father does not wish one of these little ones to be lost." (Matt. 18:12–14)

The story verges on the impossible, leaving ninety-nine to the elements, thieves and wolves to go after just one that has strayed.

Sheep are easily disturbed, especially without a shepherd. They make a great deal of noise but don't know what to do when they are frightened. Someone in Ireland told me of returning home to his family's farm after years away.

Late at night he finally got into bed to sleep, exhausted from the transatlantic flight. But he couldn't sleep for the noise all night outside his room. The sheep had been penned in earlier that day, and they were making a din. Early in the morning he got up and went into the kitchen and asked what in the world was wrong with the sheep—the bleating and whining and crying all night long. The family laughed and told him the sheep had been sheared that day, and the lambs couldn't recognize their mothers and the mothers couldn't recognize their little ones. Sheep are indeed dumb!

So Jesus' story of the lost sheep is as much hyperbole as the exhortations in the sermon that immediately precedes it. Just as the effects of sin witnessed by others is so drastic, the work of the Good Shepherd going after these lost ones is drastic too. What has been done to them, the harm they have experienced at the hands of others, is remedied by the shepherd himself going after them in their pain and distress. The joy over one sheep, one sinner who repents and returns, is echoed in heaven itself (Luke 15:7). Traditionally, this joy is the joy of the angels breaking forth in delight that one of the little ones led astray by his or her brothers and sisters has been brought home and is now safe. This is the work of Jesus, the Son of Man, the Lamb of God, and all those who call themselves his followers. The early Fathers of the Church speak often of the angels rejoicing at the salvation of any one, especially one who is not considered important in the world, for such a person is crucial to the full joy and full complement of the kingdom of heaven.

Each of us, small or great in the kingdom, has been given an angel at birth. The early Fathers of the Church have many descriptions of guardian angels: protectors, superintendents, overseers, assistants, herdsmen and shepherds as well as guardians. The primary shepherd or guardian of the sheep, of course, is Jesus, the Good Shepherd, the Son of Man. But the angels are given to each human being to accompany them on their journey to the kingdom of heaven. The tradition is clear: the angel is entrusted with the person at birth, but at baptism the angel's role becomes more specific and indeed is an altogether new work. They are guides, beginning in the catechumenate, and after baptism assist in instruction, remembrance of belief and "protect the soul against troubles from within and without; they reprimand and punish the soul that turns aside from the right way; they assist it at prayer and transmit its petitions to God." These three functions are designated by the Fathers of the Church under three titles: the angel of peace, the angel of penitence, and the angel of prayer.[1]

These functions are fulfilled by all guardian angels but it is the Angel of Peace especially who protects voyagers: "We pray to God who is well disposed toward men in order that He might give an angel of peace as a companion to protect us." Anyone who labors to attain salvation for us—neighbors, companions, others—are considered angels of peace according to Gregory of Nyssa. The protection is specific: to protect the soul from the temptations and actions of others such as sin, scandal and allowing evil to occur unchecked in the world. They are companions in the midst of temptation and danger. St. Athanasius, in the *Life of St. Anthony,* says, "The vision of the angels works softly and peaceably, awakening joy and exultation" (p. 75).

The early Church teaches that catechumens especially are subject to attack by demons and others who seek to keep them from baptism. Sometimes these hinderers are their own family and friends from their past life. Psalm 90 is the prayer for anyone who is subject to hesitation in doing good and continuing the journey of faith and growth in virtue: "For he will command his angels to guard you in all your ways" (v. 11). This angel, who can be called upon in times of need, is also the Angel of Penitence. He teaches the believer how to resist sin and hold the power of evil at a distance, as Jesus did in the desert when he was tempted by Satan. The Angel of Penitence brings hope for all those who repent and are converted to the gospel as a way of life that saves not only themselves but others who witness their resistance to evil and their practice of good, especially in times of persecution and injustice.

Origen speaks about the Angel of Penitence, who guides those who have the care of souls: confessors, spiritual directors, counselors, bishops, when they teach the Church on moral and ethical issues, all those who play a part in healing the soul from the effects of sin. He speaks of the innkeeper in the parable of the Good Samaritan as an angel who took the coins of the Samaritan and cared for the one injured on his journey until he could return to check on him. These angels tend those sick physically, mentally and spiritually. The stories of Jesus being tempted in the desert note simply that when the temptations were finished, "angels ministered to him" (Mark 1:13) and "angels came to serve him" (Matt. 4:11).

These angel guardians and healers comfort and strengthen human beings in their struggle against sin in their own weaknesses and in the world at large. The long tradition of spiritual direction and growth in virtue is that there are two angels for each human being: one of justice and one of wickedness. Hermas, the Shepherd, describes them:

> The spirit of justice is mild and reserved and meek and peaceful. When he enters into your heart, he speaks at once with you of justice and modesty and temperance and kindness and pardon and charity and paternal love. As often as these thoughts arise in your heart, know that the spirit of justice is with you.... Now learn the works of the spirit of wickedness too. First of all, he is irritable and bitter and rash, and his works are evil. When you recognize his works, depart from him (p. 80).

This influence of evil and good angels, one of justice and one of iniquity, continues the story of the struggle between good and evil, a combat that echoes the powers of the world and the reality of the cross in our lives and in the world. The conflict is experienced on a small scale in all human beings' lives. Our guardian angels are with us for two works: to restrain us from sin and doing evil, especially giving scandal to others, and to incline us toward good and the practice of justice and the corporal works of mercy and virtue. The angel of good is always the stronger of the two, in spite of the evil in the world. The issue is: Do we trust good, risk and hope? Or do we cling to what is at hand?

Angels and hospitality, the hard work of resisting evil, guardians of our souls that seek our good and the restoration of humanity: these are all interconnected. The work of being human is the work of being united in one heart and mind and living in community. We who once were far from God have been brought close in the person of Jesus. We are to go forth and draw into our homes and hearts those who are still far off. This is the work of redemption, of salvation, shared with us. Jesus tells us, "As the Father has sent me, so I am sending you" (John 20:21). This command to go forth comes with the peace of Christ and the abiding presence of the Holy Spirit, guardian of our souls. We are not alone in our journey. God is hospitable to us always and sends angels to attend and minister to us. Hospitality to strangers, attending to the needs of travelers, immigrants, the homeless, exiles, outcasts, strangers, even enemies in our midst is the work of angels. It is the way to return the favor of God to others along our way.

Henri Nouwen in *The Wounded Healer* tells a simple, stark story of inhospitality and the drastic and destructive effects it has on the community.

- A young fugitive comes to a remote village. It is in the midst of war, and there is pillage and hatred between factions. The soldiers come, hunting him down. They threaten the villagers if they do not hand him over to them. Everyone is afraid. They go to the local minister of their church and ask him what they should do. He turns to the Bible and reads the verse: "It is expedient for one man to give his life for the people." And he tells the people to hand the young man over to the soldiers, who torture and kill him.

That night the minister goes to bed and an angel comes to him, asking why he turned the man over to the soldiers. The angel says, "Didn't you know that he was the Messiah?"

The minister is horrified. "How was I supposed to know that?" he questions the angel.

The angel says: "If, instead of reading your Bible, you had gone to where he was hidden and looked into his eyes, you would have known"[2]

If only...If we hear the words of our elders: "Be careful what you say. You never know when you are talking to an angel." Or if we listen to Paul in his letter to the Hebrews: "Do not neglect to offer hospitality; you know that some people have entertained angels without knowing it. Remember prisoners as if you were with them in chains, and the same for those who are suffering" (Heb. 13:2–3). The mystery of the Incarnation tells us to be careful, be watchful. We do not know who accompanies us and who seeks to be our friend, angel and protector. The basis of hospitality is trust of strangers—and angels—in our midst.

NOTES

1. Daniélou, *Angels and Their Mission*, 73.

2. Adapted from a story recounted in Henri Nouwen, *The Wounded Healer* (Garden City, N.Y.: Doubleday, 1972), 25–26.

8

ANGELS, STARS AND DREAMS OF CHRISTMAS

Angels we have heard on high, sweetly singing o'er the plain,
and the mountains in reply, echoing their joyous strain:
Gloria in excelsis Deo,
Gloria in excelsis Deo.

There is a very famous story told around Christmas time. It was probably one of the first stories I ever heard and years later could still tell, though I thought I had outgrown it. It is called "The Littlest Angel."

- Once upon a time, there was a very little angel. He hadn't grown up much and had not yet been assigned to anyone. He was still learning his way, playing on the star-strewn floor of heaven and listening to the conversations of older angels and the choirs of heaven. It seemed that they were learning a new song lately, one that he had never heard before. He would get lost in it and sometimes fall asleep.

  One day he was eavesdropping on a conversation that the Archangel Gabriel was having with some of the choir. Gabriel said, "Tonight is the night we have long awaited. Tonight we go down to earth, to the fields outside Bethlehem, to the shepherds tending their sheep, and we sing to them: 'Gloria!' I want each of you to go and choose those who will come and sing with us."

The littlest angel so hoped to be chosen, but doubted he had a chance. He was so small, and he couldn't sing very well yet. He could barely fly. He looked down from heaven and searched again for the place that the Archangel Raphael had once pointed out to him: Bethlehem, where the Christ child was to be born. He thought to himself, Maybe if I started out right now, I might get there by nightfall, even if I do fly so slowly. He wanted a gift to give the child, and so he quickly ran around and collected a handful of star flowers. Then he headed down to earth. Earthlings, he already knew, valued star flowers as symbols of hope fulfilled.

So he went from star to star, stopping for rest when he became tired. It was easy at first, but then he jumped from the last friendly star and there was still a long way to go in the dark below. He jumped again and landed on the hard earth. Now, which way to Bethlehem? It was different down here. He looked about and headed toward the light, a village. He walked now, but it was harder here on earth.

In the late afternoon light he came to a stop. He heard a sound: *cheep-cheep-cheep.* He looked down at his feet, to find that a bird had fallen from its nest. He bent down and picked it up and brought it back to its home. He dropped a star flower beside the rescued bird, not even noticing, and a bell rang out. He was surprised by the sound, but he saw no one and went on his way.

The angel reached the edge of the village, one of the poorer houses with the door ajar. Inside he saw a careworn mother sitting beside a fevered child tossing in pain. The child saw the angel and smiled. Then it fell into a peaceful sleep. The angel bent over the cradle and dropped some star flowers onto the child. There was a double peal of bells.

Now it was darker. His feet were bruised, and he was too tired even to try flying. Then he heard angels in the distance. Was he going to be too late? And then, closer by, he heard a lamb bleating. He stopped and saw that its fore-leg was broken. He consoled it, picked it up—and dropped the last of his star flowers. Now he had no gift for the child. The lamb in his arms bleated. It knew home was nearby. The angel saw a cave and thought it would be a good place to rest for a while.

The angel went into the cave with the lamb in its arms and saw a woman and her child. The child smiled and the woman listened to his story. She comforted him and told him that he'd already brought a better gift than all the star flowers of heaven. He had cared for creatures that needed comfort and solace. Then the child reached out for the lamb and touched it, and the lamb jumped from the Littlest Angel's arms and frisked about on the floor. The child laughed in delight. The woman laughed too and said, "This night you, by your good deeds, have rung the golden chimes of charity—already three times they have rung out. That was the signal for the choir of the angels to begin their Gloria! And now, every Christmas it will be your work, your privilege, to visit earth and send music through the hearts of those who are good and open-hearted to those in need."

And so the Littlest Angel flew back to heaven that night utterly spent and utterly happy. And every year he returns to earth to fulfill the woman's command.

Listen to the bells, the chimes of charity. Do charity and help the Littlest Angel to sound it through the waiting world, and leave behind a star flower honoring the Star Child of the universe.

The story is anonymous; it belongs to everyone and everyone tells it in a personal way. It is a story first of Christmas, of the Child and Mary and only then a story of angels. In the Middle Ages there were many stories that mixed angels, stars, charity, the hopes and dreams of the waiting world and the dark that was shattered by the creatures of light in choirs. In fact, many believed that stars, dreams and angels were all the same, one reality expressed in differing forms and symbols. Christmas is full of stars, dreams and angels.

The story is mysterious and fraught with wonder. The woman gave birth to a son, her firstborn, wrapped him in swaddling cloths and placed him in a manger because there was no place for them in the inn. But after the birth the marvelous events begin. Unlikely witnesses, the first to hear the good news of salvation and Jesus' incarnation are shepherds camping in the countryside, keeping watch over their flocks. Shepherds were considered a bit shifty, possibly thieves, by those who dwelled in the city. Even though David had been a shepherd before he was king, and promises were made of one who would shepherd his people Israel with a staff of righteousness, still, plain shepherds did not fare too well. The story begins abruptly (the way angels have a tendency to just be there, where there was nothing before):

> Suddenly an angel of the Lord appeared to them, with the Glory of the Lord shining around them.
>
> As they were terrified, the angel said to them, "Don't be afraid; I am here to give you good news, great joy for all the people. Today a Savior has been born to you in David's town; he is the Messiah and the Lord. Let this be a sign to you; you will find a baby wrapped in swaddling clothes and lying in a manger." Just then the angel was surrounded by many more angels, praising God and saying, "Glory to God in the highest; peace on earth for God is blessing humankind." (Luke 2:9–14)

These are the angels of the Nativity, the Christmas angels. It seems that angels appear most often at the beginning and end of the life of Jesus: at his incarnation and birth and again at the resurrection and ascension. They are transition times, times of coming and going between heaven and earth. The places of entrance and departure are full of angels. They are the messengers of good news, signals for those open to hope and a possibility of salvation for all peoples. First Zechariah sees Gabriel, then Mary. Traditionally, it is Gabriel who comes to Joseph in a dream, and it is Gabriel who comes to the shepherds and inaugurates the song of the Gloria. But this song, announcing the presence of the Holy One as child among the poor, must be sung and shared among many. It is to the poor, beginning with the shepherds, that the good news is given. The shepherds are the first to hear of the Shepherd of Israel: "And you, Bethlehem, land of Judah, you are by no means least among the clans of Judah, for from you will come a leader, the one who is to shepherd my people, Israel" (Matt. 2:6).

This is the prophecy text quoted to King Herod when the wise men come from the East searching for the newborn king. They have seen the rising of his star and want to honor him. Their arrival strikes fear and rage into the present king, Herod, living in Jerusalem. He meets with them privately and questions them about the star and the child, and then he sends them to Bethlehem with instructions to return to him with information. He intends to kill the child. So evil also attends the birth of this child, along with dreams and stars.

The child and his parents will have need of angels, stars and dreams to escape the rising tide of evil and hatred that is set in motion by his birth. When the wise men leave the city of Jerusalem the star went ahead of them and stopped over the place where the child was. Then they have dreams of warning and go home by another route, avoiding King Herod. These dreams come to the wise men, and later to Joseph, like angels: demanding, imperious and with such surety that Joseph and the wise men act upon the knowledge imparted as hurriedly as the shepherds do when they decide to go to Bethlehem in response to the song of the angels.

When the child is safe and on its way to growing up, the stars, dreams and angels cease. They appear again at the start of Jesus' public ministry, after he is tested in the desert, and then again at the dawn of resurrection life, for Jesus the Christ and for all humankind.

The angels hover within places of danger and possible death. The boundaries of space, time and history merge between the forces of this world, which often deal in death, and the powers of heaven, which are intent on giving life. Those who can see angels also see a child born to poor parents as the Messiah and Lord. Joseph and the wise men also begin to recognize evil and danger. It is knowledge that is crucial to the survival of the child and its guardians.

When there is hate, menace, plots to kill, death and the disruption of hope, the angels, stars and dreams abound. Who is friend and who is enemy are clearly marked. These are messengers not just to individuals for their enlightenment but for the whole human community. They are intertwined with the salvation and oppression of peoples, the lifting of affliction and the coming of blessings upon those who hope for peace. When there are drastic threats against the providence of God and those who obey God, an angel goes before and leads the people toward safety and refuge until the danger is past. These aren't merely private revelations but necessary for the future of humanity, a future of grace and freedom.

The angels can represent peoples, nations, tribes and whole generations of people that wait in hope. In the Jewish communities, each nation had an angel to guard it, even the enemy nations of Israel. Michael is the protector of the people of Israel, but there are others, and at the birth of the savior of the world, all the angels of all the nations gathered to exult and rejoice that at long last the Holy One had begun his work on earth, the work that would redeem the fallen world and recreate it anew. The angels remind us that all the world serves God and all creatures of the earth and heavens are bound in this task and gift of salvation.

The glory of the Lord shone around the shepherds, much as the cloud engulfed the Israelites on their journey through the desert and the cloud overshadowed Jesus on the mount of the Transfiguration and the Spirit overshadowed Mary at her surrender to the Angel Gabriel's request from God. These experiences take human beings outside themselves and into the larger community of human beings, into a deeper truth of communion. And as soon as the angel leaves, the star disappears, the dream is over, it is imperative to act on the knowledge that has been opened up. For a few moments in a night of praise and wonder, a night of silent Word descending, a night of worship and adoration and giving of gifts, a night of amazement and stories told by shepherds about a child's birth, there are angels and the presence of God, the mysterious enveloping presence of holiness nearer to earth, breaking the usual boundaries of heaven and earth. Deliverance is sung aloud, psalms of glory ascend and descend and even despair and the madness of evil cannot touch what is sung about.

Joseph heeds his dreams and takes Mary and the child and runs into exile in the land of Egypt, the old land of bondage and oppression. The moment of birth and its joy and gifts of innocence are quickly wrenched and twisted by the realm of evil. The family that guards the child who will shepherd his people with justice quickly becomes one of millions of refugees from political intrigue and destruction vented on the powerless.

The United Nations Commission on Refugees and Immigration says that at any one time, one-third of the world's people is homeless, on the move. They desperately search for a place to rest, to be safe and to live without misery and murder as daily occurrences. Today we only have to look at Bosnia, Africa, Vietnam, Cambodia, Haiti, Mexico, Central America and the borders of the United States to see the tide of those running today just as the holy family ran then.

A familiar Christmas hymn calls forth the response that is demanded by any angel's presence in our world as the guardian of the weak:

> It came upon a midnight clear,
> That glorious song of old,
> From angels bending near the earth
> To touch their harps of gold.
> "Peace on the earth, good will to men

From Heaven's all-gracious King,"
The world in solemn stillness lay
To hear the angels sing.

This world of history, this earth battered long by wars, nationalism, small terrors and petty sins, is beleaguered and tired, in need
of those who walk by starlight, make dreams come true in the day-
light hours and know that the presence of angels is not primarily
for one's own protection or gain. Angels are for larger issues of
hope, for bringing light into the stifling air of despair and for
escape when necessary from the evil human beings can do to each
other. There is an old saying to heed and take heart from: Only
those who walk in darkness ever see the stars.

The good news to the poor, the birth of God in human flesh, does
not always engender joy and delight. It draws forth rage and hatred
intent on once again derailing the hopes of God for all creatures.

In the Middle Ages, the night of Christmas was often seen as a
night of confusion for demons and the angels that had fallen. It dis-
oriented them and threw them for a loss. What they had feared,
what they had refused to bend before and so lost forever—the presence of God—was coming true in the world and they couldn't stop
it. God had broken through and the kingdom of peace with justice
was a reality that could never more be undone. It was truly a night
of glory and wild delight. But it was the beginning of danger for
those allied to the Child, the Lamb of God. He would see the rising of the darkness against his light, and one day evil would snuff
out his life in betrayal, murder, crucifixion and death. Still, the
night of Christmas and the dawning of the day star signaled a new
era of choice and allegiance for all on earth.

There is a story of Christmas that I do not often tell. It is personal, and it is full of mystery and strangeness. Every time I tell it,
I wonder again and reflect on what I am to learn from it. It is a
story of "Ah, what if..." and of great sadness, because of failure and
lack of wonder, lack even of simple kindness on a Christmas night.

• Once upon a time, about ten years ago, I lived in Mission San Antonio, one of the few California missions still belonging to the Franciscans. It was my first year there, along with three others. We sought to be a presence of hope and prayer, for the mission was situated in the middle of Hunter-Liggett Army Airforce Base, which was used as a training ground and practice area for dangerous missions and the testing of new weapons. We gave retreats to groups, especially to those who were physically and intellectually disabled, who are rich in insight and wonder that never cease to teach us wisdom. It was our first Christmas together, and we had decorated and cooked for weeks. Many of the young people stationed at the base had been coming to mass on Sunday and staying for breakfast, and the numbers had grown. In addition, we had invited novices from the communities in the outlying cities, friends and neighbors. Midnight mass was packed, and the singing and lights in the old church set the tone for silent and deep rejoicing. It was a magical night.

Afterward, folks stayed around. It grew late, around three in the morning. There were many rooms in the mission, enough to sleep fifty people, and some had decided to stay the night rather than drive back to San Francisco in the dark on the back roads. We were in the kitchen cleaning up and putting food away, happy, tired and content, when one of the friars asked me: "Did that man ever come and ask you if you'd seen his friends?"

I looked at him blankly, not having a clue what or whom he was talking about. He told a story of a man, dressed rather poorly, who had come to the mission just after mass. He was looking for his friends, who were supposed to meet him here. He said the woman's name was Maria, but he had forgotten the name of the child. He was tired and hungry, probably one of the many "illegals" who lived on the property that belongs to the United States government, hiding there even though the terrain was used for demonstrations of live ammo and military exercises. It seemed that practically everyone had seen and talked to him. The last person had seen him within ten or fifteen minutes, but oddly, no one knew his friends, and worse still, no one had offered him food or even hospitality for the night.

Finally, I asked: "Did he say what his name was?"

"Yeah," my friend answered. "He said it was Gabe."

I looked at him peculiarly. And he looked back. We were both thinking the same thing: Gabriel—looking for a woman named Maria and a child on Christmas night. Both of us reacted fast—No! it couldn't possibly be. But all four of us who lived at the mission ran for the car. It had only been a few minutes since he had been seen heading down the road off the base. We knew there were only two roads out of the base, and both of them had gates and guards at the end of them. In both cases it was fifteen to twenty miles before the main highway. We could catch him.

We took one road. We drove fast, lots faster than the speed limit. Not a sign of him. We backtracked and took the other road, less frequented, all the way out to the highway. Not a sign of him. We drove back to the mission in complete silence. We got out of the car and finally separated, going to our own beds for the rest of what remained of Christmas night.

As I went into my hall, I turned to my friend and he whispered: "Do you think it was really them?"

I didn't reply for a while and then answered, "You know, it really doesn't matter whether it was them or not. We blew it. On this night of nights, we missed the presence of the poor, of those who are the dearest friends of God, looking for shelter and a home, some warmth and human companionship, a place to share food and rest with friends." I cried all the way back to my room.

To this day, I wonder—Gabe? Gabriel? the angel of the Gloria slipping among us once again. How disappointed the angels must have been that cold, clear night in California. Never again, I vowed, never again. That Christmas and every one since then I remember and know that the presence of angels, even the rumor of angels, is blessing and benediction, but it is also judgment and revelation. It exposes human kindness—and human selfishness. Even Christmas is about the need for salvation, refuge and redemption. We will be judged on what we do for the lost children among us.

The story echoes Jesus' reminder to his disciples: "Know that the Son of Man will come in the Glory of his Father with the holy angels, and he will reward each one according to his deeds" (Matt. 16:27). It is not a comforting thought.

The angels of the Nativity, those attending the birth and the early childhood of the One long awaited, seem like doorways between one reality and another. In many parts of the world people speak of the veil between realities, and that it is thin in certain places. There are places of revelation, of insight and profound conversion, much like Saul's conversion on the road to Damascus. There is a story in the Book of Numbers that speaks of this kind of seeing. Oddly enough, it may have connections to the stories of Christmas. It is about a donkey and an angel.

Balaam is paid a fee by the king of Moab to put a curse on the Israelites. That night, Balaam is visited by Yahweh, who tells him not to put a curse on the people because "they are blessed." The next morning Balaam refuses to go with the Moabites, even though they send more and more men of distinction and authority to plead with him. Finally, in another dream, Yahweh tells him to go with them, but to do only what Yahweh tells him to do. And so Balaam saddles up his donkey and goes with the delegation to the king. Yet God is angry, and an angel is posted in the road, a drawn sword in his hand.

Balaam was riding on the donkey, and his two boys were with him. When the donkey saw the angel, she turned off the road and went into the field. Balaam hit the donkey to get her back on the road. But the angel of Yahweh stood on a narrow lane between vineyards with a stone wall in either side. When the donkey saw the angel of Yahweh, she shrank against the wall, crushing Balaam's foot, so he beat her again.

Then Yahweh's angel went ahead and stopped at a narrow place where there was no room to go either to the right or left. When the donkey saw Yahweh's angel there, she lay down under Balaam; he was angry and beat her with a stick.

But now Yahweh opened the mouth of the donkey and she said to Balaam, "What have I done to you to make you beat me three times?"

Balaam answered, "You have made a fool of me. If I had a sword just now I would kill you."

And the donkey said to Balaam, "Am I not your own donkey that you have ridden to this day? Have I ever dared to do this to you?"

He said, "No!"

Then Yahweh opened Balaam's eyes, and he saw Yahweh's angel standing on the road with a drawn sword. He bowed and fell downward, his face to the ground. Yahweh's angel said to him, "Why did you strike your donkey three times? I have come here to oppose you because you are going a wrong way. The donkey saw me and turned away three times. Otherwise I would have killed you, but not her."

And Balaam said to Yahweh's angel: "I did not want to sin. I did not know you were posted against me on the road. But if this journey displeases you I will go back."

Yahweh's angel said to Balaam, "Go with these men, but you may say only what I tell you." So Balaam went on with Balak's men. (Num. 22:22–35)

The story seems fantastic. Dreams of Yahweh come to a seer from the land of Babylon, a sorcerer who makes his living cursing enemies. Even when he dreams of Yahweh and is told not to curse the Israelites he still goes forward; after all this is his living. And his poor donkey, caught between a rock and a hard place, sees the angel immediately. Every time she seeks to avoid the sword of the angel she is beaten severely by her master. And then the donkey speaks, which doesn't seem to surprise Balaam. The donkey points out that she has always been a good and faithful donkey. It is wrong for Balaam to beat her so mercilessly. And Balaam's nature is revealed in his answer to the donkey: "You've made a fool of me."

Yet in reality, the donkey has saved her master's life three times. Balaam is blind to everything but his own profit and stubbornness. It is Balaam who is the donkey!

Then Balaam's eyes are opened and he can plainly see the angel of Yahweh, sword in hand. The angel takes the part of the poor donkey and questions Balaam on his treatment of the animal. And Balaam pleads ignorance, that he didn't know Yahweh was opposed to his journey. Now he sees.

Three times Balaam is shown the Israelites' encampments in various places and told to curse them; instead, he blesses them. This infuriates the Moabite king, who pleads with him at least not to bless them. But Balaam has learned his lesson, and his path is clear; he can only bless those whom Yahweh blesses. Once he has seen the angel and heard Yahweh's voice, he can only obey. And in the end, he gives an oracle to the nation of Moab:

> "Word of Balaam, son of Beor, the seer, the one who hears the words of God, who has knowledge from the Most High, and sees the vision of the Almighty, in ecstasy, with eyes unveiled. I see a figure, but not really. I behold him but not near. A star shall come forth from Jacob, he rises with a staff in his hand; he shatters the forehead of Moab and tears down all the sons of Sheth. He conquers the land of Edom, and takes the cities

of his enemies. Israel grows strong; Jacob dominates." (Num. 24:15b–19)

It is Balaam who announces the "star of Jacob" and the "one who rises with staff in hand." This one, of course, is David, the great king to come generations later, but this star of Jacob who rises with staff in hand is always the Messiah, the child who will shepherd the people of Israel and all the nations on the earth.

In this legend there are elements that surface often in the legends and stories of Christmas. The boundaries between animals, angels, humans and creation blur; some can cross them, some can see across them and some cannot. In this case, Balaam cannot see but his donkey can, his donkey being more in tune with the ways of Yahweh. It is the donkey that saves Balaam's life three times, even though her owner punishes her for it.

In Christmas legends there are stories of donkeys that dream of laying aside their burdens and carrying kings, of escaping their masters and knowing freedom. The tales tell of the innkeeper's daughter who takes her father's donkey and lends it to Mary and Joseph for the journey to Egypt, carrying the burden of mother and child freely, rejoicing to be part of saving the child from the sword of King Herod. The donkey's dreams are surpassed.

There are countless other legends of animals, flowers, stars and other creatures of the universe being able to see the child, knowing that this is the night of nights, and going to Bethlehem to pay their respects and stand in awe around the manger. On this night all of creation that obeys and waits on the word of God can transcend the boundaries imposed by time, history and sin. The simple and poor of the earth, together with the choirs of heaven and the dumb animals rejoice that salvation draws nearer in the birth of this one child.

St. Augustine wrote that "every visible thing in this world is put in the charge of an angel." And there is this Jewish saying: Behind every blade of grass is an angel, singing "Grow, grow, grow." And just as creation suffered as evil began to spread through the world, now it knows the healing balm and coming sense of peace that this child brings to earth. The land itself rejoices at his coming.

> The wolf will dwell with the lamb,
> the leopard will rest beside the kid,
> the calf and the lion cub will feed together
> and a little child will lead them.
> Befriending each other, the cow and the bear
> will see their young ones lie down together.
> Like cattle, the lion will eat hay.
> By the cobra's den the infant will play.
> The child will put his hand into the viper's lair.
> No one will harm or destroy over my holy mountain,
> for as water fills the sea
> the earth will be filled with the knowledge of the Lord.
> (Isa. 11:6–9)

Jesus brings enduring peace with justice to all the inhabitants of earth who are of good will and to all the creatures of earth as well. It is the magic of Christmas that, at least on this night, all is well and the earth is a dwelling place secure, even for the beasts of the field and creatures of no account.

The simple dream of St. Francis of Assisi sparked the legends of the Christmas crib and the gathering of the animals into the cave, along with the angels and the church. All fear is laid to rest in the manger and hope begins to sprout as the Christmas rose.

It is not so strange that the one who made the stars and taught them their songs, who set the boundaries of water, air, sky and land, would loosen those boundaries by grace and freedom so that once again all creation could play before his face. These are intimations of the coming fullness of resurrection, which this child set in motion, destroying even the hold that death has on humanity and creation. He shatters all the boundaries. But for now, the angels of the Nativity teach those who have the eyes to see and hearts large enough to see what is already in our midst. These angels are musicians in concert with the stars of the universe. They are friends to all the great and small creatures of the earth, who know all the same songs. They sing to all human beings who are simple and true enough to hear: all of those who seek after peace and the knowledge of the Lord. The message of these angels, devastating to many on earth, is "Peace on earth to all of good will. Peace on earth now."

_____

9

MINISTERING ANGELS WHO TEST, JUDGE, RECORD AND REVEAL

The angels keep their ancient places;
Turn but a stone; and start a wing!
'Tis ye, 'tis your estranged faces,
That miss the many-splendoured thing.
　　　　—Francis Thompson "The Kingdom of God"

C. S. Lewis has told a story, often adapted, that is both funny and hard to take. It reveals sides of us we often avoid.

- A senior devil is instructing a group of neophyte demons in the ways of misguiding human beings. He asks them what methods they plan to use to lead humans into sin. One demon tentatively mentions the temptation of atheism; if people give up their belief in God, he points out, they are easy for the devil to guide into the path to hell. The senior devil agrees, but points out that this method doesn't always work all that well. People have a tendency to hedge their bets and in situations of disaster or fear or war, they return to God and beg for help. What other methods are there?

  Another demon responds that there is the temptation to believe there is no hell; then people can concentrate on themselves and the pleasures they want without fear of an

_____

"accounting" in the future. The senior devil agrees that this is indeed a good method, although with all the wars, genocide, killings, hate, and so on in the world, people are inclined to think that there just might be hell to pay!

Next a timid demon made yet another suggestion: the temptation to believe that God is so loving there is nothing to worry about. But, the senior devil says, even this method doesn't work as it used to. People live longer, and this method works best with younger people. The old think too much about their lives and about God, and they have time on their hands. The senior demon looked around encouragingly. Any other methods?

From way in the back came yet another suggestion: the temptation of no fire in the soul, no passion in the heart. Now the senior devil gets really excited. He agrees that this method is quite effective and points out that it works especially well on religious people, those who think they are basically good but are too wrapped up in themselves and their small lives. It works best where God is taken for granted and people are comfortable with their spiritualities and going to church. They go through all the motions, but their hearts are not alive with the love of God. This is certainly an excellent method, and he encourages the demons to make frequent use of it.

So off the demons went to earth, with the methods of temptation, especially the fourth one, clear in their minds.

When you read this, or sit in church with your neighbors, you might look around at all the good folk. Are they feeding you the fourth temptation? Or more to the point, are you feeding the fourth temptation to others by your words and life? No fire in the soul, no passion in the heart.

The traditions of the early Fathers of the Church, the Jewish communities around the world and medieval legends all abound with stories of angels, temptations, times of testing and the recording of deeds for the final judgment for individuals, which is separate from the judgment of the nations as described in Matthew 25 and in the Book of Revelation.

In both Matthew's and Luke's gospels, Jesus is tempted in the wilderness by Satan at the beginning of his public ministry. He is tempted with human needs and with power as it is used on earth, power that is given into the hands of Satan and then to anyone who worships him. And he is tempted with religion, with using the relationship he has with God to protect him from suffering, evil and death, rather than letting that relationship make him human and true, compassionate and trusting in God. In both accounts Jesus and Satan both quote scripture. Satan uses passages out of context, trying to get Jesus to reveal who he thinks he is and what his strengths and weaknesses are. He baits him: "If you are the Son of God, the one you claim to be, the one others will claim you are, then use that power—use that power as Satan himself would use it." The progression of the temptations escalates and extends into all areas of human life. And Jesus resists—with prayer, fasting and the word of God in scripture. He refuses to obey Satan or prove himself to him or to do anything that might offend God or put God in the position of having to respond to a test of loyalty or love. The stories reflect the early Christians, who were struggling with all the things that Jesus faced and had to decide how to live and act in a world ruled by might, oppression, greed, hatred, nationalism, racism, selfishness and idolatry. We are all faced with the same choices and temptations.

In the other gospels, Jesus faces these temptations at the end of his public ministry, at the edge of being arrested and tortured and killed as dangerous and seditious. In the garden where he goes to pray he confronts the hatred and evil of human beings that is about to be unleashed on him, and he sweats blood. He falls on his face to pray to God, in submission and obedience, in trust and fear. He bows before no other god or way of living. There is the sense in all these instances that angels minister to him, attend to him and are present to him in his struggles. What Jesus says and does is crucial to the coming of the reign of God to the earth. It is essential to his mission of good news to the poor: healing, reconciling, forgiving, doing justice. This confrontation, this standoff with Satan, is core to the living of a Christian life. We are committed to following Christ and fulfilling our baptismal promises to live in the freedom of the children of God, to resist Satan with all our strength and resources and to oppose evil individually and together as the body of Christ, the Church.

Traditionally, the angels of the Churches as well as the angels of individuals who seek to be holy and to serve the kingdom of God are present in all these encounters. In fact, in the early Fathers of the Church they are sometimes sent out to test the believers, monks and hermits and Christians, and to reveal their weaknesses and strengths. They are aids to conversion, spiritual guides, internal and external witnesses to actions and thoughts that sometimes expose the deeper and broader meaning of seemingly insignificant actions and individual lives.

- Once upon a time, there was a devoted and faithful monk. He had lived in the desert for years, first with other monks and a master, and then for many years alone. He lived a good distance from the others in order to pray better, concentrate on his penances and atone for the sins of the world. Every morning he would head off into the desert, going to the well to get his water. It was a good distance each way, about a mile, and as he grew older and slower, the trek across the hot sands became more and more of a penance. In fact, it began to be all he thought about: when he got up in the morning he dreaded it; he complained on the way going and returning; and late in the afternoon he grumbled, knowing that tomorrow he would again face the hot sands, the slow pace and carrying the heavy buckets. It was interfering with his prayer and silence. He started thinking about moving his tiny hermitage closer to the water.

One day it was especially hot and wearying, and he was trudging across the sand toward his hermitage. In his hands were the heavy buckets with his precious water. He was tempted to stop and take a drink, but that would mean that much less water when he got home. And then, behind him came a slow, steady drone of a voice: 100,002 …100,003…100,004…100,005. He stopped and turned around. Not a soul in the desert except himself. He shook his head and wiped the sweat from his eyes and continued, one step at a time. The drone picked up again: 100,006…100,007…100,008. Again he turned. A vast emptiness of sand and horizon. He was getting old; hearing voices now! He turned and began again, and the drone came again: 100,009…100,010…100,011.

This time when he turned he saw the towering figure of an angel with a book in hand, recording his steps, detailing all. They looked at each other closely. Then the angel spoke. "Keep going, don't mind me. I'm the Recording Angel, and I am keeping track of each one of your torturous steps so that they will be remembered in the Book of the Living. I don't want you to miss your reward or the grace that will accrue to others on your account. Nothing is lost—ever."

The old monk turned and plodded toward home, his mind in a whirl. The next day he moved his tiny hermitage another mile away from the well!

The story encourages us to hope, reminding us that no small detail goes unnoticed, no challenge or suffering occurs without the possibility of redemption and meaning. But the story can have the opposite effect. We may be appalled to think that every small detail is noted and taken into account, that nothing escapes the Recording Angel. Such close attention can be frightening or heartening, depending on what it is we are engaged in doing daily, repetitively, with or without awareness and intent.

Angels are sent to individuals as they examine their lives and seek to live as holy men and women in the world. This is the inner journey, where the pulls to good and evil are constant and involve every area of existence. Traditionally, it is the role of the principalities, archangels and angels to test those on the spiritual journey, aiding them and calling them to confession, conversion and repentance. They are the teachers of virtue, self-denial and purification. They are the guides for beginners in the spiritual life.

In turn, the second set of angels—dominations, virtues and powers—reveal more hidden mysteries of spirituality and prayer, illuminating those who contemplate and seek to atone for the sin of the world. And the highest orders of angels—the cherubim, seraphim and thrones—participate in and initiate the believer in the experience of union. These ministries and services sometimes are performed externally for the benefit and teaching of others, but more often deep in the hearts and souls of those who seek to obey and honor God alone in adoration and devotion. Each order deals with light, light within light within light, drawing the individual closer and deeper into the light of Christ and the Spirit and the Father—the depths of the Trinity.

The inner journey begins with purification and the doing of good deeds, the corporal and spiritual works of mercy among human beings. This first step is that of example, of discipline and of behavior toward others. It is, the stories relate, no easy task to push and prod someone onto the first steps of the path.

- Once upon a time, two shopkeepers vied in competition with each other. The rivalry grew heated and nasty until both families were involved in the pettiness and disputes. The clashes escalated, and soon they were hating each other, lying about one another and cheating to get ahead and make the other look bad. Finally God had had just about enough. So God sent an angel, Raphael, to bribe them to be human and civil toward one another again.

Raphael arrived and went straight to one of the shopkeepers. He told him how the situation saddened the heart of God. He explained that he was prepared to offer him anything—reputation, wealth, a luxurious home, prestige and influence in the community, success in business, fame, security for his family, anything. All he had to do was ask for it, and it would be given.

The man was overjoyed, even gleeful, making lists in his head, figuring the future, cackling aloud. His wife thought he was insane (she could not see or hear the angel). As he was figuring exactly what and how much to ask—how far he could push this situation—the angel Raphael added: "There is only one condition to this arrangement. Whatever you ask for, double will be given to your neighbor."

The man was furious and answered quickly. "Then tell God to make me blind in one eye."

This story reminds us that seeing an angel doesn't always result in goodness or holiness or grace for the human race, or even for the person who sees the angel. The angel's words and actions reveal the depth of the human heart and its evil as well as its good.

Stories operate on an individual level and on a more communal or social level as well, affording whole groups a chance to reevaluate their ideas and philosophies. This theme of pushing people to see, to repent, to change their minds and hearts is repeated in story again and again. In medieval morality plays, the devil goaded his minions to punish the people in a hell complete with pitchfork and flames and the screams and cries of the punished. Then the "harrowing of hell" would be proclaimed joyously by a choir of angels. Jesus died on the cross on Good Friday and went straight to hell and set free all those who had waited and were faithful: the ancestors in faith, the prophets and kings who were just, the children of Israel and all those who looked for God. The devils would shriek as hell was emptied. With few souls left to torment and torture, Satan himself went into mourning. Then God would comfort Satan: "Don't worry, there will be others soon enough. As soon as the self-righteous and religious people find out what I've done, you'll have a full house again. Unfortunately, there are many who want justice for others but mercy for themselves." Satan would begin to dance and cavort around again, and God would sternly remind him: "Remember, though, I will come again, with justice and with mercy."

Such stories may seem foreign to our ears but they echo the gospel accounts. Jesus often confronted the people of his day, not just the scribes, Pharisees and teachers of the law. Luke's gospel recounts the story of Jesus driving out a demon from a person who was mute; when it was gone, the person could speak. Some of the people immediately accused him of driving out demons by using the power of Beelzebub (Satan), and others were shocked and amazed. They didn't believe in him and sought "to put him to the test by asking him for a heavenly sign" (Luke 11:16). Jesus knew their thoughts and spoke of division and factions as signs of the devil. He asserted that he drove out demons by the finger of God, and that his very presence and power said that the kingdom of God had come among humankind. He said to them: "Whoever is not with me is against me and whoever does not gather with me, scatters" (Luke 11:23). It was a time to choose.

A woman later interrupted Jesus and cried out that he was blessed and so was the woman who bore and nursed him. But Jesus' reply revealed another reality: "Surely blessed are those who hear the word of God and keep it as well" (Luke 11:28). This is what saves.

"People of the present time are an evil people. They ask for a sign but no sign will be given them except the sign of Jonah. As Jonah became a sign for the people of Nineveh, so will the Son of Man be a sign for this generation. The Queen of the

South will rise up on Judgment Day with the people of these times and accuse them, for she came from the ends of the earth to hear the wisdom of Solomon; and here there is greater than Solomon. The men of Nineveh will rise up on Judgment Day with the people of these times and accuse them, for Jonah's preaching made them turn from their sins, and here there is greater than Jonah.

"No one lights a lamp to hide it; rather he puts it on a lampstand so that people coming in may see the light.

"Your eye is the lamp of the body. If your eye sees clearly, your whole person benefits from the light; but if your eyesight is poor, your whole person is without light. So be careful lest the light inside you become darkness. If your whole person receives the light, having no part that is dark, you will become light, as when a lamp shines on you." (Luke 11:29–36)

The angels, creatures of light, are interested, like Jesus, in spreading the light, in illuminating the world and those who dwell in it. Those who ask for signs are blind, without faith. Those who believe do not ask for signs; they rely on the word of the Lord and act upon it. The visits of angels that test, reveal, record and judge serve the light of the world. They are horrified at what some of those who call themselves children of the light, followers of Christ, do so self-righteously, selfishly and glibly.

Jesus tells his disciples to pray: "Pray that you may not be put to the test" (Luke 22:40). He reminds them three times in the garden to pray with him, and then he returns to pray alone, kneeling on the ground: "Father, if it is your will, remove this cup from me; yet not my will but yours be done." And an angel from heaven appears to give him strength. Then Judas comes into the garden with the soldiers and goes up to Jesus and kisses him. Jesus is arrested, and the disciples scatter. Peter follows at a distance, soon to betray Jesus publicly and vehemently, and the others all flee in fear, leaving Jesus in the hands of those who hold him in contempt. They have all failed the test, individually and as a group.

Jesus is adamant in his preaching that hearing the word and putting it into practice are essentials. The initial enthusiasm of belief must be built on strong foundations of both doing good and resisting evil or else it will all come to naught. He speaks of judgment:

> Not everyone who says to me: Lord! Lord! will enter the kingdom of Heaven, but the one who does the will of my Father in heaven. Many will say to me on that day, "Lord, Lord, did we not speak in your name? Did we not cast out devils and perform many miracles in your name?" Then I will tell them openly: I have never known you; away from me, you workers of evil! (Matt. 7:21–23)

Often when angels appear to believers and those in religious positions it is to prod them to examine their assumptions and behavior and to grow in understanding the word of the Lord and in putting it into practice; they are warned not to rely on their past and their outward practices of religion to save them. Angels come to break patterns, to warn, to share wisdom, to encourage the practice of justice and the care of the poor. They come to connect a specific instance in a person or a community's life to the larger vision of salvation history, the long-range vision of God. In this sense they are single-minded and single-hearted, relentlessly preaching obedience to the word of God.

There is a delightful story told in Ireland of a blacksmith, a good man who worked at his trade and cared for his family and neighbors:

- There was nothing extraordinary about the blacksmith or his life. Then one day he had a vision. An angel came to tell him that God was coming to call him home to the kingdom of heaven.

The blacksmith responded: "Please, tell God that I am grateful for his thinking of me, but I can't go right now. You see, it is time to plant the crops. I'm the only blacksmith for miles around and the people need me. I must stay. They'll need shoes for their horses, plows sharpened, hoes and rakes and shovels fixed. You see, I have to stay. Could the Lord put off my coming home to the kingdom until the planting season is finished?"

The angel left and returned quickly. Yes, the blacksmith could stay. And the blacksmith went about his business, serving his friends and neighbors.

After the planting season the angel came again. "Are you ready?" the angel asked. "It's time to come home."

Once again, without hesitation the blacksmith responded. "Oh, could we wait on this? My next door neighbor is so sick and his family is in dire need. I've promised to take in his crops and care for his children. If I go now, they will suffer so much more. I'm sure if you explain about this, God will understand."

The angel vanished and quickly returned. Yes, it could be arranged.

Of course the angel came again and again. But the blacksmith always had a good reason to delay: an especially hard year, a famine, a drought, neighbors in need. The blacksmith gently reminded the angel that there was so much need and that his presence could ease some of the suffering. Finally, for a long time, the angel gave up coming.

But eventually the angel came again. This time the blacksmith was old and tired—just plain worn out. He was overjoyed to see the angel return. Now he was ready and willing to go. In fact, he'd been praying to God to send the angel. The angel smiled at him, and the blacksmith said, "Am I glad to see you! If God wants to take me home now,

I'd be delighted to see the kingdom of heaven at long last and find my place in his bosom."

Then the angel looked at him and laughed.

Confused, the blacksmith looked at him. Then the angel said: "Good servant of the Lord, where do you think you've been living? You've been home for years now."[1]

The kingdom of heaven has strange borders. Humans sometimes can cross over them as angels do, though often we do not know where we are. The mystery of the coming of the Holy One into the world says that now even the presence of those who believe and put the word into practice in the world can draw heaven down to earth and lift earth up to heaven.

NOTE

1. I have used another version of this story in my book *Parables: The Arrows of God* to illustrate Jesus' teachings on mercy.

10

ANGELS OF RESURRECTION AND REVELATION

As it was in the beginning, is now, and will be forever.
Amen.
Who, if I cried, would hear me among the angelic orders?
—Rainer Maria Rilke

Much of what is sensed in beginnings is only truly appreciated in endings. This is true in stories, individual lives, epochs of history, family experiences, and so too in the life of Jesus. Especially in the life of Jesus. He was born of the Spirit's invitation to a woman of Nazareth; adopted by Joseph of the tribe of David; brought good news to the poor and ushered in a kingdom of enduring peace with justice; was crucified, died, buried and then raised from the dead. Just as angels attend his birth in the back country of Galilee, angels attend his breaking forth from the tomb outside the city of Jerusalem and his ascension into heaven from a hill outside the city. The angels ascend and descend, accompanying him. Endings, especially one as layered with meaning as Jesus' dying and rising, are doorways between realities, in this case between earth and heaven, human and divine, time and eternity, death and birth. Life takes its meaning in the in-between.

There is a story from before World War II, a Jewish story from Eastern Europe that was often told to new immigrants when they arrived in the "promised land" of the United States after the war.

The events occurred in a small synagogue in a small village in Lithuania. The synagogue and the village no longer exist, except in memory and in long-lost bones and dreams. The story's name is "The Weeping Synagogue." It is as good a place as any to look at seeds planted at beginnings that finally come to bear fruit in revealing and powerful ways.

- Once upon a time, there was a rabbi. He was a holy man, compassionate and concerned about his people, and he passionately loved and studied, prayed and preached the Torah. He lived in hard times, but, they say, no harder really than other hard times.

  Late at night the old rabbi could be found bent over his study table in the light of a flickering gas lamp, researching and praying the words of Torah. One night very late, long after midnight, as he was studying, there was a voice in the synagogue: "Rabbi, I am an angel of the Lord, sent to bring you a gift from heaven." Then there was silence.

  The rabbi looked around and saw nothing. He rubbed his eyes. He was tired; indeed, the lines on the page seemed to run together. Perhaps he was overdoing it. He shrugged and went back to the page.

  Again the voice came: "Rabbi, I am an angel of the Lord, sent to bring you a gift from heaven."

  This time, even though he still saw nothing, he responded to the voice: "How do I know you are an angel of the Lord?"

  "This is a holy place, rabbi. Only that born of God or that which serves God may enter into God's sanctuary."

  The rabbi was silent and went back to his studying.

  A third time the voice came, "Rabbi, I am an angel of the Lord sent to bring you a gift from heaven."

  The rabbi pushed his books away and asked, "Why should heaven bring me a gift?"

The voice moved closer to him, in front of him, and the air shimmered like a breeze on a summer's day. The angel replied: "You are a holy man, rabbi, and the Lord is pleased to give you anything you ask. On this night only, anything you ask of the Lord will be granted to you."

The rabbi's mind whirled. What should he ask for? I could ask for money, he thought. Then I'd be able to care for all the widows, orphans, strangers, the poor that come to my door. It is always so hard to turn them away empty-handed or with the small pittance I sometimes am able to give them. But after he thought about it for a while, he decided no, that wouldn't be wise. In his long life he had learned that suffering and hardships can bring out the goodness in a human being. The needs of fellow human beings were meant to evoke compassion and pity in the hearts of those with more than they needed. No, he would not ask for that.

He thought again. What if I ask for long life, time to contemplate the wonders of creation and praise God on myriad more Sabbaths? I would have time to pray for so many of those who need counsel and advice and prayer before the Almighty. But then he realized all too clearly that he was old. He had already lived past the scriptural seventy or eighty years. No, he had also seen enough of evil and the destructive side of sin and humankind. He would not ask for a longer life.

Ah, he thought, I could ask for wisdom, as Solomon did. But then his glance fell upon the Torah scroll and the commentaries spread out before him on the table and he smiled to himself. What need did he have of wisdom like Solomon? Here was more wisdom than Solomon had ever known, and it had sustained him all his life. The Word of the Lord was wisdom enough for lifetimes. No, he would not ask for that.

Finally he raised his eyes and spoke surely and clearly to the angel, "Angel of the Lord, please tell the Holy One, blessed be his name, that I am honored that he would give me such a blessing and offer me such a gracious gift, but I have no need of anything. The Lord has provided me with so much. I am humbly grateful for all his gifts, and there is nothing that I lack or am in need of. In fact, there is nothing that I desire. I am content."

There was silence, long, hard silence, and the rabbi wondered if the angel were still there. There was no glimmer of light, no shimmering, no sound.

Then the angel of the Lord spoke in a voice loud and terrible, the voice of one who is horrified and appalled: "Rabbi, you are a stupid and selfish man. You may be holy and compassionate to those in need who come to you, but you are nonetheless a stupid and unthinking man. The Holy One offered to give you anything that you asked for and you, in your selfishness, refused God's gift. You could have asked for anything! You could have asked for no more hunger or disease or war upon the earth, no more hatred. You could have asked for the victory of right over might. You could have asked for the Messiah to come! Anything at all, and all you could think of was your miserable life. What a disappointment you are to the Almighty and to all the earth that waited on your word this night." And the angel left him.

The next morning when the people arrived for the morning service they found the rabbi lying near death on the stone pavement of the synagogue. They revived him only long enough for him to tell the story of his terrible experience and how he had failed them and failed the nation because he could not think past his own small world. He died and before sundown was buried under the stones of the room where he had studied and prayed for so many years. During the service there was the sound of mourning, weeping, keening and terrible grief. It frightened the people, and they said among themselves that it was the rabbi mourning his sin and failure to save the earth.

Every morning and evening after that, during every service the mourning continued and even grew more intense. Soon people stopped coming to the synagogue. They couldn't bear the sound in their ears or the memories and hopes that had died inside them with the rabbi's story and failure. Eventually they boarded up the synagogue and put a lock on the gate. With the passing of time, grass and weeds overtook the courtyard and out of fear people walked on the other side of the street.

Yet at night and in the early hours of the day the people could still hear the rabbi weeping. The sound was wrenching, full of despair and loss. Some said it wasn't the rabbi weeping, that the Holy One, blessed be his name, had long ago forgiven him for his selfishness. They said it was the angel of the Lord, who was disconsolate, weeping still for the message that he had had to deliver to the Holy One. They believed the angel's heart and spirit were broken.

Later the war came and the small village and the synagogue and all its inhabitants were destroyed, wiped from the face of the earth by horror and inhumanity. But the story was carried in memories and voices that had visited corners of hell on earth. It was told again and again to those who went to other shores. It was told as warning, as remembrance and in hopes that never again would such a possibility be lost, that if a gift were given again by the Holy One the same terrible mistake would be averted.

Immigrants came to the "promised land" with wild dreams that anything could happen—freedom tasted, hope renewed, families reunited and started in love and devotion, and God always praised and honored here in this place. But always the story concluded with these questions: Whom do your dreams exclude? Whom do they forget? How small is your world? How small is your love and mercy? Do you have only your own dreams or do you dream the dream of the Holy One, who desires life for all? Do not give the angel any more cause to weep if it is up to you to respond to the gift of the Holy One.

The story has much to say of revelation and resurrection and how hard these realities are for humans. We set boundaries. We limit hope and shrink dreams. We are disbelieving of the promises and covenants of God. We lose hope and slip into a world of cynicism and despair; we begin to believe and to act as though the world is not held in the hand of God. Even those who are the companions of God, God's beloved children, who are dear to God's heart, get trapped in meanness of spirit and lack of imagination. The rabbi in this story is kin to all of us.

In Mark's gospel there is a resurrection angel with great news. He is described as "a young man sitting on the right, dressed in a white robe." He is inside the tomb, with the great stone rolled aside, and the women who come to anoint the body stumble not into death's domain but an empty hole in the earth that once harbored God's presence. The angel's message is fantastic:

> "Don't be alarmed; you are looking for Jesus of Nazareth who was crucified; he has been raised and is not here. This is, however, the place where they laid him. Now go and tell his disciples and Peter: Jesus is going ahead of you to Galilee: you will see him there just as he told you." (Mark 16:6–7)

The announcement of the resurrection is mind shattering. How can we not "be alarmed"? Alarm seems to be a natural reaction to finding an empty tomb with an angel residing within. Jesus was laid in the tomb as he was laid in a manger so long before: temporary resting places. The tomb was really the womb of God, and now Jesus has burst forth into the world. It will have to reckon with him again. He goes before his friends into Galilee, as he has always gone before them, into suffering and persecution, death, healing, praying, preaching and teaching. Now, he shows the way into a life of spirit and a presence stronger and more alive than any known before on the earth. His disciples will see him there, as he promised. The angel reminds them of what they have forgotten in their grief.

The women run, beside themselves with fear. Fright has torn away their words. They say nothing to anyone because of their fear. The presence of the angel in the tomb paralyzes them. It drives them out of grief and into something even more terrifying—a life they never imagined and can't comprehend. They are seized by the unknown, the unexpected and the wild recognition that perhaps nothing will ever again be the same.

They are caught in their mourning and weeping, their self-recrim-inations, despair, loneliness and cramped worlds. They miss the pres-ence of Life itself, when Life is trying to stretch them, body and soul, and tickle their minds into joy. Like the rabbi in the story, they need to break boundaries, break into a belief that will never cease to expand. It will include more of Life, the Holy One's presence and power let loose in the earth through the hallowing of death.

Matthew's account is very different. Mary Magdalene and the other Mary go to visit the tomb after the Sabbath is over, and they see what happens at the tomb.

Suddenly there was a violent earthquake: the Angel of the Lord came down from heaven, went to the tomb and rolled away the stone from the entrance of the tomb and sat on it. His face was like lightning and his garment white as snow. The guards trembled in fear and became like dead men when they saw the Angel.

The Angel said to the women, "Do not be afraid, for I know that you are looking for Jesus who was crucified. He is not here, for he is risen as he said. Come, see the place where they laid him. Now go at once and tell his disciples that he is risen from the dead and is going ahead of you to Galilee. You will see him there. This is my message for you."

> They left the tomb at once in holy fear, yet with great joy, and they ran to tell the news to the disciples. (Matt. 28:2–8)

In this account the women see the angel appear from heaven and open the tomb. Only the women see and hear him and deal with him; the soldiers have become like dead men. Later the soldiers will be bribed to keep quiet by Jewish authorities. The angel's presence and message cause the women to run, but here it is with a holy fear that is more reverence and awe, bordering on worship, and they go with great joy. They are intent on telling that the Crucified One is now gloriously alive. And on the way Jesus meets them, as he did so often in life.

In Luke the women come to the tomb at dawn. There seems to be a good number of them who had followed him from Galilee and had watched the crucifixion from a distance. They find an opened tomb and no body. Then they see two angels dressed in dazzling clothes who appear to them.

> In fright the women bowed to the ground. But the men said, "Why look for the living among the dead? (You won't find him here. He is risen.) Remember what he told you in Galilee, that the Son of Man had to be given into the hands of sinners, be crucified, and rise on the third day." And they recalled Jesus' words. (Luke 24:5–8)

Now there are two angels, and their presence causes the women to bow. The angel reminds them of the mission of the Son of Man and encapsulates the essence of faith. Then they remember hearing the good news, the words of the Master they had followed from the beginning.

In John's gospel it is Mary of Magdala who goes to the tomb in the dark. She sees the empty tomb and runs to the disciples. They run to check what she has said and then go back home again. But Mary stays by the tomb weeping, caught up still in her grief. As she weeps she bends down and looks inside the tomb. Now she sees two angels in white sitting where the body of Jesus had been.

"Woman, why are you weeping?" She answered, "Because they have taken my Lord and I don't know where they have put him." (John 20:13)

Mary answers matter-of-factly. She is obviously immersed in grief. She continues to talk to the angel, telling it that she will take the body if she just can find out where it is. Jesus himself speaks to her, and she doesn't recognize him. She is too wrapped up in her own pain and loss. It is not until Jesus calls her by name that she recognizes him. Even the presence of two angels doesn't break through her grief. But then Jesus asks her the same question: "Woman, why are you weeping?" Perhaps the question is meant to situate her more in the present, away from the past reality of death and into the presence of the One who fills the earth with life.

All those who see angels are grasped firmly by the experience and wrenched out of their personal emotions and relationships into another reality that is communal. They are sent to others, as angels are sent, to question, to announce, to declare a new order of existence, to stretch the boundaries of belief and hope and love.

The angels of resurrection ease the transition between one form of life and an altogether other form of life that has been set in motion by the resurrection. We know nothing of the angels' own sense of the resurrection. We perceive them intent on bridging gaps, rolling stones away from death, airing out tombs, calming fears, getting Jesus' disciples and followers ready for the shock of seeing him again, alive. Their glorious appearance is nothing in comparison to his appearance in glory, the glory of God that transfigures him so completely that even when he is seen, he is not immediately recognizable.

These angels of resurrection are intermediaries, dragging a straggling community into a new place where Jesus can appear to them and send them into the world as he was sent into the world by the Father. They accompany those who are believers and prepare the way before the risen One. These angels will appear again at the ascension, when Jesus is "taken up before their eyes and a cloud hid him from their sight." Those gathered to hear him and reverence him stand looking up to heaven, and suddenly two men dressed in white stand beside them and ask, "Men of Galilee, why do you stand here looking up at the sky? This Jesus who has been taken from you into heaven, will return in the same way as you have seen him go there" (Acts 1:9–11).

Now the angels move believers between the presence of the Holy Spirit in the world and the coming of the kingdom here on earth to the time when the kingdom will come in fullness when Christ comes again. The Son of Man descended to earth and ascended to heaven, and he will come again in glory. These words echo prophecies about the Son of Man found in the gospels: In Matthew, Jesus tells them: "Know that the Son of Man will come in the Glory of his Father with the holy angels, and he will reward each one according to his deeds" (Matt. 16:27).

Earlier in Matthew's gospel Jesus has explained a parable about judgment to his disciples:

> "Just as the weeds are pulled up and burned in the fire, so will it be at the end of time. The Son of Man will send his angels, and they will weed out of his kingdom all that is scandalous and all who do evil. And these will be thrown in the blazing furnace, where there will be weeping and gnashing of teeth. Then the just will shine like the sun in the kingdom of their Father. If you have ears, then hear." (Matt. 13:40–43)

Angels are the workers, the gatherers of all souls, those who separate weeds from wheat and execute the judgment. Theirs is the work of punishment and reward, executed in obedience to the presence of the Son of Man.

In the Book of Revelation an angel is sent to John to give him hope and courage under persecution. John's visions will help the Churches to endure evil, horror, torture, exile and death. It is a time of martyrs and apostates, life and death, good and evil, truth and sin. It is a crucial time, a time of great faith and great betrayals. It cries out for direction, for long-term meaning and angels of hope.

The visions come "from Jesus Christ, the faithful witness, the first-born of the dead, the ruler of the kings of earth." All the nations of the earth will mourn his death. Yes. It will be so (Rev. 1:5–7).

John sees the visions and is told to write them down in a book and give them to the seven Churches of Ephesus, Smyrna, Pergamum, Thyatira, Sardis, Philadelphia and Laodicea. All the visions are seen in the context of the description of the one who speaks to John:

> I turned to see who was speaking to me; behind me were seven golden lampstands and, in the middle of these I saw someone like a son of man, dressed in a long robe tied with a golden girdle.
>
> He touched me with his right hand and said, "Do not be afraid.... Now write what you have seen, both what is and what is yet to come. Know the secret of the seven stars you saw in my right hand and the seven golden lampstands; the seven stars are the angels of the seven Churches and the seven lampstands are the seven Churches." (Rev. 1:12–20)

The speaker is "like the son of man"—the traditional description of an angel in the Hebrew scriptures. But this one declares he is the Christ. And the stars are the angels of the seven Churches.

What follows is a letter to each angel of each Church detailing its failures and strengths. The letters are couched in the language of battle. The historical background is a time of relentless persecution, martyrdom and death. The Churches are reeling from the destruction visited on them by the powers of the Roman government. It is a battle for bodies and souls. Each letter is a fervent call to conversion, to single-heartedness and dedication to the gospel and to the fullness of the kingdom here on earth. The letters are full of hope, consolation and power for those who have the ears to hear and the heart to put them into practice.

After the letters there are visions of the end-times. These visions are filled with angels who sing God's praises without ceasing and also carry out the destruction of the earth, separating those who are saved from those who are not. And then there is the great vision of the wedding feast of the Lamb, of the reign of God in glory and the gathering in of the holy ones of God who have remained true. Now the angel commands John to write of joy, of expectations fulfilled, of glory given. "Write: Happy are those invited to the wedding of the Lamb…. These are the true words of God" (Rev. 19:9). And when John falls at the angel's feet to worship him, the angel warns him: "Beware, I am but a servant like you and your brothers who utter the testimonies of Jesus (these testimonies of Jesus are proclaimed through the spirit of the prophets). Worship God alone" (Rev. 19:10).

Here the angel of the Book of Revelation reveals what angels really are: they are the servants of God, like all of us who seek to be faithful witnesses to Jesus as Lord of heaven and earth. Angels, like humans, are commanded to worship God alone. In their essential natures, human and angel are united in worship, obedience, servanthood and adoration.

With that warning to John the end arrives. The battle is finished, though history has long aeons ahead of it to face the struggle. The ultimate end is justice, judgment, the chaining of Satan and all those who follow him and the opening of the Book of Life. "Then the dead were judged according to the records of these books, that is, each one according to his works" (Rev. 20:12). All are judged; we are either found in the Book of Life or we are not.

The angels in the Book of Revelation are numerous, too numerous to count. They represent Churches as well as nations, even periods of history. These angels sing, cry out, attend to God alone, worship God alone, obey every command and wish and desire of the Holy One. They exist, they watch and they give thanks. They wield the power and authority of God and share it with those who are faithful, seeing themselves in league with those who remain true, especially in the face of suffering. They always direct humans toward God's mysterious plan. They announce the presence of God and praise the Holy One unceasingly, welcoming all to join them in their songs of glory. They are links between heaven and earth; they visit earth and yet somehow remain before the throne of God. With them, space and time are blurred.

The angels are God's messengers. They stand against all unnecessary suffering and death and stand witness to martyrs and the little ones of the earth who are victims of massive evil and injustice. They take note of all that is done in the name of God or in subservience to idols. They abhor malignancy and inhumanity and all that does not reflect God in creation and in humankind. They are sent to help us honor the image of God in all of creation and to bring to completion the mysterious plan of God. They attest with the prophets to what makes us fully human: righteousness. "But Yahweh Sabaoth will be exalted when he comes in judgment; and the holy God will show himself holy in his righteousness" (Isa. 5:16). And by recording and witnessing all that is done on earth even now, they participate in the judgment of the righteous and the evil. They, like the Messiah, the Christ, are intent on encouraging repentance and conversion, on making holy the world and advancing the coming of the kingdom of God in justice and peace for all on the earth. They worship and reveal the delight of creation that, like God, "every morning it is renewed" (Lam. 3:23).

Angels are servants of life and joy in spite of their connection to judgment and destroying forces. They live wrapped around God, unself-consciously, empty of all that is not the Spirit of God. They are created, like us, and yet they know that in the fullness of time we will be set above them, even though they are creatures of light and intelligence and the power of God that we cannot know now. They are made of brightness, of the stuff of stars and galaxies, and are often interchangeable with these entities.

Angels appear and vanish, come and go without warning, obeying only the will of God. They are ministers of truth, conveying knowledge and wisdom that are crucial to the human community, and they minister especially to those whose actions and lives have import far beyond their own concerns. They protect from evil and are especially near to those who do battle with injustice, systemic evil and sin. They are companions with those who choose to stand with God, the Crucified One, those who fall into the hands of sinners and those who wash their robes in the blood of the Lamb. They accompany those who love life but give up even that precious gift to stand before the truth of God and stand against anything and anyone that is tied to the death of the world.

They sing and so are often depicted with musical instruments and as a choir. They are traditionally believed to sing without words but with sounds and voices charged with purity and obedience and utter wonder. The Hasidim of the Jewish community fashion their songs, their *niggun*, melodies without words, to sing the praises of God in imitation of the angels' music. And yet the mystics and saints believe that the Holy One is still partial to the voices of human beings in the sound of compassion, shared pain, prayers for the relief and deliverance of others, and especially when voiced in repentance, contrition, cries for forgiveness and mercy and justice.

There is a story told of Moshe Leib of Sasov that reminds us of what God wants to hear:

- The good rabbi died and he said to himself: What am I to do now. The commandments of the Lord apply only to the living. How do I fulfill the will of the Holy One now? He thought about it and in an instant decided: I am sure that the will of the Holy One is justice, and so I must atone for my breaking of his commandments and my failure to honor him in works and words before the nations. And so, before the angel at the gates of heaven could judge him, he ran and with all his strength threw himself into the fires of hell.

Immediately there was havoc in hell and chaos in heaven. What was going on? Word went forth from heaven: "Stop the fires of hell. There is someone there who should not be there." The angel who kept the fires burning obeyed and soon spotted the rabbi. The angel came to the rabbi and in the name of the Almighty petitioned him to get himself out of hell and into the kingdom of heaven. But the rabbi refused. The angel argued with him. The balance, the order of the universe was off. He was out of place. The fires of hell had ceased while he was in them.

The rabbi thought about this for a moment and realized what kind of power he had. And so he informed the angel: "In that case, I'm not leaving, not until all the souls suffering in such torment here get to come with me. After all, what did I do on earth but obey the command of the Holy One, blessed be his name, to release the captive and to set free all those held in bondage? There is much work to be done here with this great hoard of souls. After all, the Holy One Himself told us: 'I am the Lord your God who took you by the hand and lead you out of the land of Egypt, out of bondage and into the land of promise.' I must continue to obey the command of God."[1]

It seems that those made in the image and likeness of God, like his beloved Jesus, cannot bear the suffering of even the unjust and are willing to share that suffering and atone for it until somehow the harmony and order of the universe are restored and all are reconciled with God.

Suffering and misery profoundly disturbed the prophets, and it seems that they disturb the angels as well. The angels, like God, cannot close their eyes to human misery and the evil that we do to one another as we destroy the image of God in our brothers and sisters. Martin Buber has a short story called "The Angel and the World's Dominion" that describes an angel who cannot bear the sufferings of humans below on earth:

- An angel comes before the throne of God and begs God to entrust to him the ordering and care of the universe for just one year, so that he can change the basis for living and lay new foundations for the future of the world. He intends to ease human misery and stop the horror that is done on earth. The other angels are surprised, even appalled by the angel's audacity, but the Creator is pleased and grants the angel his wish. He is given one year.

  The angel moves swiftly throughout the world, "and so a year of joy and sweetness visited the earth. The shining angel poured the great profusion of his merciful heart over the most anguished of earth's children, those who were benumbed and terrified by want. The groans of the sick and dying were no longer heard in the land. The earth floated through a fecund sky that left her with the burden of new vegetation. When summer was at its height, people moved singing through the full, yellow fields; never had such abundance existed in living memory. At harvest time, it seemed that the walls would burst with the plentitude of the crops."

  The angel is delighted, proud of his work. He returns to heaven sure that the work he set in motion will benefit the children of earth for many years to come, perhaps even generations. The domain of the earth reverts to the hands of God.

  The next year begins and the cries from earth also begin. They are in anguish, despair, pain beyond reckoning. The angel is frightened. What could possibly be wrong? He goes down to earth dressed as a pilgrim and roams the land, stopping at houses and villages as he goes, and what he learns overwhelms him. The people are besieged by horrible sufferings. The grain they use to make flour into bread has no substance. It is uneatable, with a terrible sour taste that is bitter, like dirt or clay. The people are starving and are in despair thinking that God gave false blessings to them. The angel returns to heaven and falls before God in tears; with great cries of lamentation he cries to be taught, to be given understanding. What did he do wrong? He only meant to ease the burden of the human beings, and it seems that he has added to their misery and caused them to test God and to sin in despair at their sufferings. And so God raises his voice and speaks to the despairing angel: "Behold a truth which is known to me from the beginning of time, a truth too deep and dreadful for your delicate, generous hands, my sweet apprentice— it is this, that the earth must be nourished with decay and covered with shadows that its seeds may bring forth—and it is this, that souls must be made fertile with flood and sorrow, that through them the Great Work may be born."[2]

The angel is loved; he is called "my sweet apprentice." But he is taught the hard truth about being human. It is the mystery of the cross, of the seed falling into the ground so that it may bear fruit. It is the mystery of redemption, of dying and laying down one's life for others. In fact, the angel as pilgrim and compassionate companion to human beings has crossed over the line between angel and human. Perhaps now he is also apprentice to the Son of Man and his followers, who share his dismay at the sufferings of earth, especially those that are not necessary.

This difference between the angels and humans is captured in a poem by Christina Rossetti called "In the Bleak Mid-Winter." It is a Christmas poem that extends this idea of being able to comfort, to ease, to share the burden and glory of being human.

> Angels and archangels may have gathered there,
> Cherubim and seraphim thronged the air;

But his mother only, in her maiden bliss
Worshipped the beloved with a kiss.

Angels are given as grace in time of strife and as guidance in the face of the Adversary. But it is God who redeems, and God has chosen to share that work with humans. It is a tradition of the Jewish community that there are thirty-six just ones, the *Lamed-vov*, who are ordinary people, often unnoticed, who preserve the earth from destruction and the human race from despair. Their lives of holiness and faithfulness are what sustain the universe. The belief is that if only one of these thirty-six should die without being replaced, then the world would sink into such misery and darkness that it would be crushed and humans would know the full weight of justice.

It is the hearts of the *Lamed-vov* that hold back the waters of the Abyss. When the pressure grows too great to bear, then the heart of one of the *Lamed-vov* breaks and another picks up the burden.

It is much like the command of Jesus: we must begin by denying our very selves, picking up our cross and following him. We are called to bear one another's burdens and to witness to the presence of God among the poor and in opposition to the powers of the world.

If there is any one work of the angels that is specific to them in relation to us human beings it is to lead us home, to restore through obedience to the will of God the original harmony of the universe. There is an ancient Jewish story that I heard long ago and tell whenever I can. It has several names; one is "The Angels' Song."

- Once long, long ago, in fact long before human beings were created, all the creatures of the world were beginning to be fruitful and multiply and to move out across the face of the earth in obedience to the word of the Creator. There was all manner of beasts and birds, of things that crawled and squirmed and moved. There were creatures no longer seen or heard of, some that now are found only in legends or in the mind's eye. There were three of these great creatures who were friends. The first was Behemoth, a great beast, strong and powerful. The earth rocked and rumbled when he walked, and when he ate he consumed huge amounts of grass. Behemoth lived near a mountain that provided food for his needs, and he drank deeply from its spring, which was ever flowing. He lived in a great cave.

His friend Ziz was a bird unlike anything seen now. She had wings that could reach from one end of the sky to the other, with great shining feathers. It was she who protected the earth from the heat of sun and wind. At night she would come and wrap her great wings around her friend Behemoth, and they would sleep soundly.

The third friend was a creature of the deep, Leviathan, a huge fish, sometimes called a monster because of his great size. He had many eyes and his scales were like rainbows glittering in the waters. When he was playful he would flash his fins and tail and cause tidal waves and great floods. When the darkness came, Leviathan would come up close to the mountain and curl his tail around his two friends, and they would sleep together.

The angels were their friends too, and the angels would sing them lullabies so that they would have sweet and dreamless sleep.

All the animals and birds and fish and crawling things were trying to get used to each other, and frankly, some of the smaller things were having a really hard time of it. The song birds would dart about looking for places for their nests and places of rest and security, trying to feed their little ones, but they were in constant peril from the predatory birds: owls, hawks, ospreys, eagles, condors. They would swoop and glide and rob their nests. It was a dangerous life and hard, too hard.

On the land there was the same problem. All the small creatures—rabbits, ferrets, beavers, squirrels, mice—hid in their burrows and in crevices and cracks, often running for their lives when they ventured out to eat. The great animals hunted them relentlessly. Wolves in packs, lions, tigers, panthers, all the great cats and bears were after them. The deer, gazelle, zebras and giraffes were also hardpressed and in danger.

In the waters of the world, from small ponds, lakes, streams and rivulets to the great seas it was the same story. All the little fish, the minnows, trout, salmon, and others, were eaten by the big fish—sharks, barracudas, rays.

Spirits, sprites and nymphs played with creation's patterns. They bent rivers to their whims and turned mountains upside down and twisted trees out of shape and changed the buds on plants. All was chaos. The earth was in turmoil and distress as each creature tried to find its place.

Finally the small and the weak ones could take no more. They called for a great gathering of all the little ones that walked and swam and flew and crawled. They came together and complained. "This is not what the great Creator of all had in mind," they said. "We were not meant to be hunted and eaten and destroyed, with no time and rest with our families and the next generation. This has to stop." There was a noise of twittering, squawking, meowing, chittering and murmuring such as never had been heard. What could be done to make life easier for all?

They spoke in safety under a great sheltering tree, near a stream. The wise ones said: "We know that some of us must be eaten and that the bigger ones must be fed, but we have no rest. We are hounded day and night. Many of us will soon disappear if this doesn't stop."

Finally, a small starfish spoke up. "I have seen great beasts and creatures. There are three of them: a bird, a beast of the land and a beast of the sea. They are friends, and every night the angels sing them to sleep. Maybe if we go to them they can help us."

And so a delegation was sent—the starfish, the mouse and the sparrow—to speak on behalf of the small of the earth to the great creatures who dwelled at the end of the world.

They found them by the great mountain, just as Ziz, Behemoth and Leviathan were about to sleep for the night. The three little ones sang to them: "Please, O great ones, hear us. Don't go to sleep. We need your help."

The great ones listened to their complaints and the story of distress upon the earth.

The little ones told of being hounded to death, with no respite and no escape, how the great animals, birds and fish were after them all the time and how the sprites and unruly spirits were creating havoc with the rivers, trees, plants and even mountains and valleys. There was no stability, no security anywhere in the world. They spoke of their fear of being erased from the memory of the earth and of the Holy One being disappointed at what was happening. They were sure that it was not God's will that they live like this. "Please, can you help us?" they begged.

The three friends looked at each other and were very quiet. Then they turned to the angels that sang to them and took counsel. They didn't go to sleep that night, and there were no songs or lullabies. They spoke among themselves and finally came to a decision: "It is time for the Great Words." This last line was whispered as a prayer, as a warning, as a decree that would have awesome consequences. The angels agreed: it was time.

They turned to the little ones and sent them on their way with reassurances that they would do something to ease their lives. The little ones hurried back with the message to the rest of the small creatures of earth, sky and water.

Time passed, and then Behemoth moved. He left his cave and went across the lands, the ground underneath him shaking and rumbling. He stopped, and he roared to the heavens. The great cats and bears, the wolves and hunters of the earth stopped in their tracks and sought to cover their ears. They lay down on the ground and hid their heads between their paws as the sound of Behemoth struck deep into their souls. The song went on, and then it was quiet. And for three months the great cats and bears, beasts of field and steppe, rested and did not hunt. For three months the mice scurried about, the rabbits danced and the little creatures darted about playing, eating and setting up their burrows and tunnels and nests. They lived and rejoiced.

Then Ziz flew from the mountain. Over the land she went, her great wings flapping. Then she cried out, sending her voice across the heavens, shaking the clouds and rending the air in ripples and patterns that resounded everywhere on the earth. And the great raptors and birds of prey all stopped, stunned, and dropped from the sky. When they did fly again their sounds were different. They did not cry out and hunt and swoop and dive after their prey, but they left off hunting and, for the first time, learned pity for the weak ones. This lasted for another three months, and the song birds, nesting birds and wading birds breathed easier and lived securely in the air and where they nested.

And then it was Leviathan's turn. He moved once again into the depths of the oceans and moved his fins and tail and set in motion a humming that echoed in the gills and hearts of all the great fish. It was like thunder underwater, and all the killer fish were stunned and still. They stopped their eating and hunting. Three months passed again, and the little fish swarmed and fed and reproduced and filled the waters of the land and seas. There was peace in the seas, on the land and in the air.

Last, the angels moved out across the earth, and they sang a song without words. It seeped into every crevice and under every stone and through the woods and fields. And the lesser spirits and sprites desisted from their mischief and left the earth to its own pattern and rhythms.

Finally, there was peace in all the universe. The year had turned and the course of the universe was set for all time.

They say that in that year all the birds of the air, fish of the sea, animals of the land and even the sprites of the universe learned a new song that they sang together. The time of words had begun. There were just four words to the song: first was Behemoth's, which was *peace*. Next came Ziz's word, which was *justice*. Then followed Leviathan's word, *mercy*. Last was the angels' word, and that word was *love*. This is the song, the psalm of creation, the *uni*-verse, the one song that encircles all the world. All that is created and sustained by the Holy One hears, listens and learns the song by heart and obeys without question. It is the way that moves through time. It is the chant of harmony, of holiness and the way creation is meant to be.

But all this happened before human beings were made and given dominion over the birds of the air, the fish of the seas, the beasts of the field and all the vegetation of the earth. So humans didn't learn the song with the rest of creation. Oh, human beings can hear and learn it by going to a place apart—near sea, under sky, on land or in the air. They will hear it if they are very still and attentive to creation. The song is never ending, all pervasive and complete. It is a holy song, and all others are found within it. But once heard and taken to heart, those who learn the song are one with all creation and know the deep truth of what is made—that all praises the Maker of the Universe by living in peace, with justice, delighting in mercy and knowing love. This is where all that is of God begins and ends.

But because the humans weren't made when the song was sung, there has been another way for them to learn it. It is called history or the mysterious plan of God. It is called hope and the cry for justice. It is echoed in songs of liberation and freedom. It is found deepest in the word *Father* spoken by the Son and carried on the breath of the Spirit. One day it will be sung in fullness again when the time is complete. The melody always begins with obedience, compassion and interconnectedness, with unity and communion. They say that Ziz, Behemoth and Leviathan and all the angels wait for that day to come.[3]

There is only one song, one word, one story, one world, one time, one history, one hope. In the beginning is found the end. John's version of the story says it most clearly: "In the beginning was the Word and the Word was with God and the Word was God; he was in the beginning with God." It is the work of this Word that the angels serve, that all born of God serve and come to know because this Word "was made flesh; he had his tent pitched among us, and we have seen his Glory, the Glory of the only Son coming from the Father: fullness of truth and loving-kindness" (John 1:14). The Word came as stranger, companion, light, truth, mercy unbounded. He put on human flesh and became our loving friend, mysteriously inviting us to honor the image of God in the face and form of every human being and with the angels to worship God alone. The angels follow him and only speak his Word. As Meister Eckhart says: The angels "abet and assist God's birth in the soul…. The soul at its highest is found like God, but an angel gives a closer idea of Him. That is all an angel is: an idea of God."

This idea of God can be absorbed and enfleshed in human folk. The saints all know this. St. Patrick in his *Lorica* prays:

> I arise today: in the might of the Cherubim;
> In obedience of angels;
> in ministration of Archangels.

And John Henry Cardinal Newman says: "An angel is a member of that family of wondrous beings who, ere the worlds were made, millions of ages back, have stood around the throne of God...and served him with a keen ecstatic love." They are, as the letter to the Hebrews says, "only servants, and God sends them to help those who shall be saved" (Heb. 1:14). They serve those who seek to grow in grace and knowledge of our Lord and Savior Jesus Christ.

There is a poem I memorized in high school by Leigh Hunt that reminds us of the one thing necessary, for humankind and angel-kind alike. This is the way I remember it:

ABOU BEN ADHEM AND THE ANGEL

Abou Ben Adhem—may his tribe increase—
Awoke one night from a deep dream of peace,
And saw within the moonlight in his room,
Making it rich and like a lily in bloom,
An angel writing in a book of gold.
Exceeding peace had made Ben Adhem bold,
And to the presence in the room he said:
"What writest thou?" The vision raised its head,
And with a look made all of sweet accord,
Answered: "The names of those who love the Lord."
"And is mine one?" said Abou. "Nay, not so,"
Replied the angel. Abou spoke more low,
But cheerly still; and said: "I pray thee, then,
Write me as one that loves his fellowmen.
The angel wrote, and vanished. The next night
It came again with a great waking light,
And shewed the names whom love of God had blessed,
And lo! Ben Adhem's name led all the rest.

Angels can learn from humankind of the priorities of God. One can only imagine the Holy One smiling as the angel obeyed and wrote another name. Perhaps the angel smiled too.

NOTES

1. Another version of this story appears in Morris B. Margolies's *A Gathering of Angels: Angels in Jewish Life and Literature* (New York: Ballantine Books, 1994), p. 196.

2. Martin Buber, quoted in Parker J. Palmer, *The Active Life: Wisdom for Work, Creativity, and Caring* (San Francisco: Harper-SanFrancisco, 1991), p. 81.

3. Another version of this story is found in Nina Jaffe, *The Uninvited Guest and Other Jewish Holiday Stories* (Scholastic, Inc., 1993).

FURTHER READING
ON ANGELS

Adler, Mortimer, J. *The Angels and Us* (New York: Collier Books, Macmillan Publishing Co., 1982).

Connolly, David. *In Search of Angels: A Celestial Sourcebook for Beginning Your Journey* (New York: Perigee Books, 1993).

Daniélou, Jean. *The Angels and Their Mission: According to the Fathers of the Church* (Westminster, MD: Christian Classics, 1953).

Davidson, Gustav. *A Dictionary of Angels: Including the Fallen Angels* (Canada and New York: The Free Press, Macmillan Publishing Co., 1967).

Eisen, Armand. *Angels* (Kansas City: Ariel Books, Andrews and McMeel, 1993).

Fontant, David. *The Secret Language of Symbols: A Visual Key to Symbols and Their Meanings* (San Francisco: Chronicle Books, 1993).

Gilligan, W. Doyle, ed. *Devotion to the Holy Angels* (Houston: Lumen Christi Press, 1990).

Godwin, Malcolm. *Angels: An Endangered Species* (New York: Simon and Schuster, 1993).

Grey, Cameron, ed. *Angels and Awakenings: Stories of the Miraculous by Great Modern Writers* (New York: Doubleday, 1980).

The Guardian Angels: An Orthodox Teaching on Guardian Angels (Canada: Synaxis Press, 1986).

Humann, Harvey. *The Many Faces of Angels* (Marina Del Rey, CA: DeVorss Publishers, 1986).

Jones, Timothy. *Celebration of Angels* (Nashville: Thomas Nelson Publishers, 1994).

Margolies, Morris B. *A Gathering of Angels: Angels in Jewish Life and Literature* (New York: Ballantine Books, 1994).

Moolenburgh, H. C. *Meetings with Angels: A Hundred and One Real-Life Encounters* (Suffolk, United Kingdom: C. W. Daniel, 1991).

————. *Handbook of Angels* (Suffolk, United Kingdom: C. W. Daniel, 1984).

Newhouse, Flower. *Rediscovering the Angels* (Escondido, CA: The Christward Ministry, 1937).

Romero, Oscar. "Sermon on the Feast of St. Michael the Archangel and All Angels (September 29, 1977)," delivered in Huizucar, El Salvador. *Publicaciones Pastorales del Arzobispado, Mons. Oscar A. Romero, Su Pensamiento* 1–11.

Vazquez, Liesl. *Angels in Our Midst: Favorite Angel Lore, Quotes, Songs and Recipes* (White Plains, NY: Peter Pauper Press, 1994).

Wilson, Peter Lamborn. *The Little Book of Angels* (Rockport, MA: Element, 1993).

————. *Messengers of the Gods* (London: Thames & Hudson, 1980).

ACKNOWLEDGMENTS

Grateful acknowledgment is made to Sister Marie-Celeste, O.C.D., of Carmel of Reno, Reno, Nevada 89509, for permission to reprint "Gabriel"; to William Hart McNichols, S.J., and St. Andrei Rublev Icons, P.O. Box 5352, Albuquerque, New Mexico 87185 to reprint "St. Joan and St. Michael the Archangel"; to Red Crane Books for permission to reprint "The Angel of Death/El Angel de la Muerte" and "Saint Raphael the Archangel" from *New Kingdom of Saints: Religious Art of New Mexico 1780–1907* by Larry Frank (Red Crane Books, 1992); and to Scala/Art Resource, 65 Bleecker Street, New York, New York 10012 for permission to reprint "Stories of Abraham and Lot: The Meeting of the Angels" by Raphael and "The Three Archangels and Tobias, before 1470" by Francesco Botticini.